DIGITAL CUSTOMER SERVICE

RICK
DELISI

DAN
MICHAELI

DIGITAL CUSTOMER SERVICE

Transforming Customer Experience
for an On-Screen World

WILEY

Published by John Wiley & Sons, Inc., Hoboken, New Jersey.
Published simultaneously in Canada.

For general information on our other products and services or for technical support, please contact our Customer Care Department within the United States at (800) 762-2974, outside the United States at (317) 572-3993 or fax (317) 572-4002.

Wiley publishes in a variety of print and electronic formats and by print-on-demand. Some material included with standard print versions of this book may not be included in ebooks or in print-on-demand. If this book refers to media such as a CD or DVD that is not included in the version you purchased, you may download this material at http://booksupport.wiley.com. For more information about Wiley products, visit www.wiley.com.

Library of Congress Cataloging-in-Publication Data

Names: DeLisi, Rick, author. | Michaeli, Dan, author.
Title: Digital customer service : transforming customer experience for an
    on-screen world / Rick DeLisi, Dan Michaeli.
Description: Hoboken, New Jersey : Wiley, [2021] | Includes index.
Identifiers: LCCN 2021024441 (print) | LCCN 2021024442 (ebook) | ISBN
    9781119841906 (cloth) | ISBN 9781119842071 (adobe pdf) | ISBN
    9781119842064 (epub)
Subjects: LCSH: Customer services.
Classification: LCC HF5415.5 .D445 2021 (print) | LCC HF5415.5 (ebook) |
    DDC 658.8/12—dc23
LC record available at https://lccn.loc.gov/2021024441
LC ebook record available at https://lccn.loc.gov/2021024442

To "The Customer":
As you have transformed to a digital-first lifestyle,
may all your Service experiences be transformed as well.

Contents

About the Authors

RICK DELISI has been researching customer service and customer experience for the past two decades. He is the co-author of the best-selling book *The Effortless Experience*, and has written several pieces that have been published in the *Harvard Business Review*. Prior to working in customer service research, he was a journalist, winning four Associated Press awards for outstanding feature reporting.

DAN MICHAELI is CEO and co-founder of Glia, the New York–based technology company that has become an industry leader in Digital Customer Service. The Glia platform helps businesses reinvent how they support customers in a digital world. He is an award-winning speaker who has been a contributor to numerous publications, including *Forbes*.

Foreword

You could say that customer service runs in my blood. My mother started her career working in the American Airlines reservation center, moving her way up through the organization before continuing on to lead customer service operations and consulting teams at companies like EDS and AT Kearney.

My first job in high school was as a telemarketer, calling people just as they sat down for dinner to ask if they wanted to subscribe to HBO (they loved me). My first job out of college was with a major US contact center outsourcer, and I've been in customer experience and contact center consulting for the last 20+ years.

Over this time, I've watched as contact center technology and operations evolved slowly and iteratively, focusing on incremental changes to minimize handle time and reduce the cost per minute of live interactions. But the rate of change has accelerated dramatically in the last six to seven years, and companies have struggled to keep up as:

- New interaction channels were added, requiring new investments and increasing the complexity, cost, and fragmentation of customer service operations
- New vendors entered the space, challenging legacy providers to "up their game" by investing in new features and functionalities to stay competitive
- Customers increasingly compared their experiences across companies – including new digital disruptors like Amazon and Zappos – raising the collective bar for all companies and industries

Enter Digital Customer Service (DCS). But what does that mean, exactly? If you asked five customer experience leaders what DCS is, you'd get five different answers and five very different approaches to how they are achieving this (or hoping to achieve this) within their companies.

DCS isn't about channel proliferation and ensuring your company can interact with customers in any digital channel of their choice. It isn't about enabling customers to do everything via online or mobile self-service. And it isn't about using bots to automate every customer interaction under the sun.

While more and more customer issues are handled (or could be handled) using self-service or some form of automation, there will *always* be a need for customers to be able to interact with a human to get the more complex and more emotive issues resolved. We call these *moments of truth* – they are the customer episodes/journeys/intents (pick your term) that have the potential to create a promoter or a detractor based on how they are handled. These are the interactions that present a rare opportunity to deepen and expand the relationship with the customer.

- DCS is about how to transform these "moments of truth" from our phone-first, analog past into a future where we leverage the digital devices that have become the omnipresent centerpiece of all of our lives, bringing a new layer of richness and depth to customer interactions.
- DCS is about truly "meeting customers where they are" by leveraging the digital entry points that customers tend to use and enhancing the interaction from there in a way that feels seamless, easy, and even delightful to customers.

Companies have been talking about seamless omnichannel experiences for years, yet few have actually achieved this aspiration, even for one-off episodes. Why is that? At the core, it's tied to the operating model of the company – namely that the digital and contact center functions tend to report up through different parts of the organization and often have competing (and sometimes even conflicting) priorities.

Until companies view their own internal processes through the lens of the way customers live their lives today, this will continue to be a challenge and a barrier to providing a truly effortless and seamless customer experience.

Digital Customer Service is for any leader who aspires to integrate digital and contact center strategies in order to take customer experience to the next level.

This book is a helpful tool for:

- Establishing a clear and common language for what Digital Customer Service is and its associated component parts
- Sizing the benefits of DCS for the company, the customer, and the frontline employee
- Developing a plan to make DCS a reality based on the pillars of an effective DCS transformation

I am personally very excited about the next phase in the evolution of customer service and how companies can transform their existing digital and customer service operations to make things better for everyone involved. This book is a meaningful step in that direction and will set the foundation for what great Digital Customer Service can and should look like.

Corrie Carrigan,
Contact Center Practice Leader at Bain & Company

Preface: Now It's Our Turn

Your call is important to us.
Due to high call volume your expected wait time is...
One. Fortnight.

Digital transformation is the ongoing integration of digital technology into *all areas of the business and culture* of a company.

This is the #1 priority for many CEOs and CIOs today. Almost all organizations recognize the need to fundamentally change how they operate and deliver value to customers. You can see examples of digital transformation reaching near full maturity in almost every area of a business:

- Just about all forms of **marketing** are now *digital marketing*. Even offline tactics like print ads, billboards and direct mail primarily drive customers to digital properties.
- In retail, there's almost no such thing as "a commercial enterprise" that doesn't include some element of **e-commerce** as well.
- Most **back-office** functionality and analytics have now transformed to become entirely digital.

But one thing we've been seeing in our research – as a collective function, **customer service** has lagged behind many others on the priority list for digital transformation.

Sure, there have been across-the-board investments in self-service functionality for company websites and mobile apps. And yes, what's been happening across the industry – adding chat, video chat, email, text/SMS communication, social media interactions – has made service somewhat more "digital."

But the differences still feel more *iterative* than *transformative*.

Here's the problem when it comes to service interactions: Not *all* problems can be solved entirely online, so it's impossible to imagine a world in which every issue and inquiry can be automated. But when customers get stuck in the middle of a **digital journey**, what do they do? They dial a *phone number* and are forced to start all over again from the beginning.

What just happened there? The customer was already authenticated in the website or app, and now they have to go through the process again. They've already indicated what their issue is while they were online, but that's all now been vaporized. They have to stop what they were already doing, find, then dial a number, push 1 for department, state their name and account number, push 3 for the category that addresses their problem – and only then do they finally reach a company rep, who asks them to start again at square one.

Live and digital service experiences are completely disconnected.

The fundamental issue here? We now live in an on-screen world. Current estimates are that during our lifetime, each of us will have spent a composite *40+ years* staring at some screen or other.[1] It's so obvious when you look at how people live their lives today.

But as "digital" as we humans have become – as natural as it is now for us to be on the internet all day, every day – how is it possible that according to estimates, companies in the US alone are still receiving over *1 billion inbound customer service phone calls* every year?

There is now a way to transform the customer experience for an on-screen world. **DCS** (Digital Customer Service) changes interactions that used to occur on the phone into experiences that take place entirely **on the customer's own screen**.

With *true* digital transformation, companies are able to start interactions using whatever communication mode the customer chooses, then seamlessly transition from one mode to another with no additional effort. But because live conversations occur on screen instead of through a separate phone call, the experience is completely different.

Live and digital service experiences can no longer be disconnected.

Transforming to a DCS strategy creates three powerful enhancements:

1. Rich automated experiences that anticipate a customer's needs
2. Rich communication options easily accessible to customers from within the self-service journey they've already started online
3. Rich collaboration tools that immediately contextualize a customer's issue, guide them through the process – and in many cases, teach them how to do it themselves next time *right on their own screen*

Companies that are well along in this transformation are reporting that they are achieving three powerful outcomes:

- Reduced cost to serve customers
- A superior customer experience
- Increased conversion rates

Digital Customer Service: Transforming Customer Experience for an On-Screen World is the roadmap for how you and your company can achieve these same goals – simultaneously.

WHAT'S HOLDING US BACK: THREE MYTHS

In this book, we'll challenge three commonly held myths about the digital transformation of customer service. These are the three primary obstacles that stand in the way of many leaders who are trying to push their organizations to rethink the way they serve customers in a digital world.

Based on the experiences of those companies that are now in the midst of this transformation, it is clear that these barriers are not as daunting – or even as true – as we in customer service had once believed.

MYTH #1: Digital Transformation of Customer Service Is All About Automation

- This means removing the "human touch" and getting out of the business of interacting and talking (verbally, using spoken words!) with customers.
- In fact, quite the opposite is true. Digital transformation of Customer Service is about using automation to empower your people to create an even more effective "human touch."

REALITY: Digital transformation is not the end of voice communications with customers. It's about using automation to employ bots to do what bots do best, so that people can do what people do best – be *human*.

MYTH #2: Digital Transformation for Customer Service Means Companies Need to Be Active in Every Available Form of Communication

- This means that companies must excel in chat, video chat, social, text/SMS, email, self-service, third-party apps, etc., on top of being great at phone communication.
- What we've been learning is that the transformation isn't about adding more **channels**, it's about curating *digital journeys*. In today's world, many of the more complex customer service journeys require a combination of virtual and human interactions in order to reach full resolution. In a fully transformed customer service operation, the options needed for each customer's specific journey are deployed automatically once that customer has begun an online session.

REALITY: Digital transformation enables companies to learn from a customer's "digital body language" exactly what kind of digital experience *this* customer needs at *this* moment. Then the DCS platform offers each person a curated journey that seamlessly transitions them from one mode to another. (This wasn't possible, until now.)

MYTH #3: Making Customer Service Fully "Digital" Seems Like It Would Be Hard or Expensive

- The companies that are going all-in on digital transformation are reporting it is easier and more efficient than they'd thought.
- These companies are not giant brand names with giant budgets, nor are they digitally native organizations that built themselves with today's digital customers in mind. They are "traditional" companies that began their service operations decades ago using a primarily phone-based platform.

REALITY: Digital transformation is surprisingly *not* hard, and there's a rock-solid ROI business case to be made for why *now* is the time to take action.

When is it going to be *our* turn to transform? The answer is: Right now, if you choose.

WHY WE WROTE THIS BOOK

We've been studying the science of customer service for the past two decades, and what we've been learning and observing is VERY exciting:

- **Rick DeLisi** has been researching the psychology of customer behavior and expectations in service for the past two decades, and is the co-author of the best-selling book *The Effortless Experience.*
- **Dan Michaeli** has devoted his career to developing solutions that create world-class digital customer experiences for "traditional" non-digital-native organizations. He is the CEO of New York–based *Glia*, a leader in helping companies reinvent how they serve their customers.

We collaborated together to explore how technology and psychology can work in concert to help companies achieve true digital transformation of their customer experience.

If any part of your job includes responsibility over the interactions customers are having with your company every day – whether you are a C-suite executive, a leader in customer service, customer experience, marketing, sales, or digital operations – this book will be immediately helpful. We will arm you with new strategic ideas as well as practical "things you can do" to increase your confidence that you *can* achieve this transformation and reap the rewards it will bring to your organization.

Our greatest hope is that the ideas we'll explore together in the pages to follow will benefit you in a personal way – both in your increasingly digital career and in your increasingly digital life. We're proud to show you what we've been learning, and are grateful you're here to share it with.

—RD and DM

All illustrations and diagrams are original works by the Glia Creative team.

One

The Problem with Customer Service and the Digital Opportunity

This book is divided into seven chapters that fit into three major sections.

In this first section, we will begin with a frank examination of *why* customer service as practiced at most companies isn't as successful as it ought to be (and why that isn't anyone's fault!), but more importantly, what you can do about it. These first three chapters are the leadoff leg of the book and have been designed to get things off to a fast start.

In **Chapter 1**, we will describe the "right now" opportunity for every company that is willing to rethink the way they serve their customers. The overall reputation of customer service is at an acute *inflection point* that will likely make or break the future success of many companies. But what we've discovered is a strategy – one that can be employed by *any* company – that appears to be creating an extraordinary confluence of positive results.

1

In **Chapter 2**, we will uncover how customer service as a collective discipline has gotten to where it is today, by tracing the evolution of our profession, starting from the days of the first call centers in the 1980s. If you've been around for a few decades, this chapter will take you back to some places you probably haven't thought about for a while. If you're a little newer to the field, it will feel like a trip to the customer service wing of the Smithsonian.

In **Chapter 3**, we will describe why digital self-service has become both the biggest opportunity and the biggest obstacle for the service profession. This is not a chapter about technology, but rather, about psychology. When you understand more about *why* customers behave the way they do when they're engaging in digital self-service (and how they feel about their interactions *afterward*), the necessity for digitally transforming service will become crystal clear.

CHAPTER 1

The Win-Win-Win-Win

What we'll share in this chapter:

- Customer service is experiencing a unique moment of opportunity. While the partial "digitization" of customer service may have sufficed in the past, now is the optimal time to take the final steps toward true digital transformation.

- Companies that are transforming customer service into an experience that takes place entirely on a customer's screen are reporting their service operations have become much more economically efficient, while they are *also* achieving greater customer satisfaction and loyalty.

- Those executives and leaders who are spearheading this transformation at their companies are recognizing an array of benefits – including making *their* jobs easier and more rewarding.

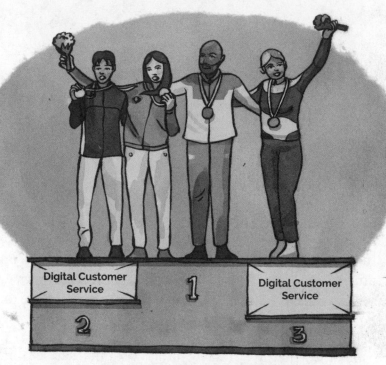

The Win-Win-Win-Win.

CUSTOMER SERVICE AT AN INFLECTION POINT

Over the past few decades, the perception of customer service has experienced a repeating pattern of ups and downs. Throughout the next few chapters, we'll trace the evolution of the prevailing **perception** of the service industry (almost like looking in the mirror) as it has **changed** several times over the past few decades – starting from the days of the first-ever call centers in the 1980s, all the way to today's digital world.

In an industry that has experienced two major peaks and two corresponding valleys – each about a decade apart – you'll see evidence that the next few years will result in *either* an unprecedented upward spike or yet another downward plunge. We are at an acute inflection point.

*The choices you and your organization make right now about the **digital transformation of customer service** will define your future success (or failure) in the years to come.*

When call centers were first introduced in the 1980s, the idea of enabling customers to call companies directly on the phone was considered new and exciting. The experience was generally excellent. But over time, as companies put more pressure on Service to cut costs, the experience of phone service began to suffer, causing the first dip.

Then, once customers got used to self-service, the experience improved and the curve rose again. But over time, as customers began to expect *everything* to be digital – and effortless – what they realized is that too many service experiences were still disconnected from their digital experiences, forcing them to restart their journey on the phone. And the phone reps they were speaking to weren't connected in any way to the digital experience customers were having on their own screens.

This mismatch resulted in disjointed "seamful" experiences that caused the second major dip.

Therefore, we are at an inflection point *right now*. If customer service embraces a full and complete digital transformation it is well within our power to rise to new heights, well beyond what we have ever accomplished before. Or, if not, to plummet once again, as we have twice before. The choice is yours, and the time to decide is now.

Who Wins When Customer Service Achieves Digital Transformation?

Based on the experiences of those companies that are now going all in, the key beneficiaries are . . . *everyone:*

- The **company,** by spending less, and getting greater returns
- The **customers** who are experiencing the kind of low-effort digital service interactions that make them feel smarter about themselves

- The **frontline teams** who interact with customers – as their jobs have become more engaging and personally fulfilling
- The **executives and leaders** who manage customer-facing functions – as their jobs have become more visibly connected to the overall success of their companies

There are only a few win-win propositions in life, and fewer win-win-win-wins. But as you will see, transforming to a DCS-based service model appears to be one of them. There doesn't seem to be any trade-off, or economic sacrifice, or give-to-get required. The companies that are further along in this transformation are universally reporting that *everyone* is coming out ahead.

THE DIFFERENCE BETWEEN "DIGITAL CUSTOMER SERVICE" AND DCS

The problem with the term **digital customer service** is that it could mean a *lot* of different things:

- *Adding a chat function to a website.* That could be described as digital customer service.
- *Switching your telephony platform to VoIP* (voice-over internet protocol). That's digital.
- *Getting customers to adopt new web self-service features.* That's customer service, and it's digital.
- *Enabling more frontline customer service agents to work from home.* That's absolutely a form of digital customer service.

In fact, you could say that anything that uses the internet to enable *any* service functionality could broadly fall into the category of *digital customer service*. And any of these could be a smart goal unto itself. Necessary, but insufficient.

The opportunity to pursue this win-win-win-win starts with understanding the clear distinction between two things that appear – at first – to be almost exactly the same: "digital customer service" and "Digital Customer Service."

The most obvious difference is: In the **Digital Customer Service (DCS)** model, every part of a service interaction happens **on the customer's own screen**. Both the "virtual" or automated elements, as well as the live "assisted" elements all take place right where they started – on a customer's desktop, laptop, tablet, or mobile device. If there's a need to verbally communicate with an agent, it becomes an entirely different **customer experience** when it occurs "right there on *my* screen" instead of during a totally separate phone call.

But the most important difference is: DCS enables companies to both "meet their customers where they are" and also to transition them between virtual assistance and live assistance in a way that is completely seamless *because it doesn't require a separate phone call*.

No additional steps are required, the customer doesn't have to do anything extra – it is a truly effortless experience.

Customers Live on Their Screens; Shouldn't You?

Even as the psychology of customer behavior within digital self-service interactions continues to evolve, what is now an irreversible trend is that customers expect and demand service interactions to take place on *their* screen.

This is the essence of DCS. What was once a disconnected experience with various disjointed elements within the span of one "journey" can now become completely integrated, and presented on a customer's own device through a variety of **OnScreen Enhancements:**

- **OnScreen Communication.** Now that most of us are comfortable using chat, video chat, messaging, and social media platforms in our personal lives, customers increasingly expect to have these same options available with the companies they choose to do business with. Whether they access the business's website or mobile app (or even when they're forced to call a phone number), using "my screen" to communicate is becoming an expectation in the digital world.

- **OnScreen Collaboration.** This set of enhancements gives an agent full transparency into what's happening on the customer's screen – in real time. It is the digital equivalent of "standing side by side" with a customer while they are on the company's website or mobile app. This includes features like **CoBrowsing,** screen sharing, and file sharing.

- **OnScreen Automation.** Chatbots and pop-up messages provide personalized responses and suggested actions on the customer's (or even the agent's) screen. These are triggered by data about *them,* from their past interactions or from their browsing behavior in that moment. Another example of automation is visual authentication, which removes that burden from agents in a way that is both more efficient and more secure.

TWO VERY DIFFERENT EXPERIENCES

To fully appreciate the difference between "a customer service interaction that includes some digital touchpoints" and a true DCS experience, it helps to envision a side-by-side comparison.

EXAMPLE

In each of these two scenarios, a customer has experienced a problem or issue that requires them to contact a company. Both interactions start the same way – with the customer visiting the company's website or mobile app. But what happens from there couldn't be more different – for the customer, as well as the agent.

Customer Service Today   **DCS OnScreen Experience**

Situation:	**Situation:**
Customer Service Today	DCS OnScreen Experience

Actions:

- Customer starts online and navigates on their own for a time.
- Eventually engages in a chat session:
  - Long delays in responses.
- Chat agent suggests a "live" interaction and provides a phone number to dial.
- Customer has to start new interaction on phone:
  - Go through IVR menu.
  - Get reauthenticated.
  - New agent asks, "How may I help you?" with no visibility into what customer has been doing.
- Customer is forced to begin process all over again.

Actions:

- Customer starts online, where they are greeted by a concierge bot.
- Customer engages in a chat session.
- Chat agent quickly suggests a voice interaction, but without having to dial a phone number, simply by clicking a button on the screen.
- OnScreen Voice agent is seamlessly brought onto customer's screen, and picks up the discussion in context (no need for additional authentication)
- Agent-facing bot provides information about customer's history and recent browsing behavior, and pre-completes forms and information.
- Customer engages in CoBrowsing with agent, who teaches customer how to complete the process on their own screen.
- Customer now knows how to complete the same process on their own next time.

(continued)

Result:
- A frustrating, discon-nected, high-effort interaction.
- Customer had to switch from screen to phone and start over.
- Even if they did get the resolution they were looking for, there was nothing about the experience that made the customer feel "special" or make them more likely to want to be more loyal to that company.
- At some level, it feels to the customer like *"that company doesn't have their act together."*

Result:
- A low-effort, loyalty-building, customer-centric experience.
- The entire interaction took place where the customer chose to start it – on their screen.
- The customer not only fully resolved the issue but feels more digitally self-reliant.
- The customer is enabled to reaf-firm the wisdom of their choice to do business with this company and is that much more likely to remain loyal for years to come.

Can you see how different these two scenarios are? In both cases, the customer got their issue resolved, but the experience is night-and-day different.

To be successful with customers who are now fully immersed in their digital-first lifestyle, companies can no longer "be OK" with service journeys that feel disconnected, disjointed, or out of touch with the way people live in today's world.

Story: "Phone" and "Voice" Aren't the Same Thing

It's the same thing. But it's completely different.

Imagine two conversations between the same two people – in this case, a customer and an agent. In both conversations, they are working together to get something done or solve some problem.

*It's the same two **people** discussing the same exact issue. But customers were describing these two kinds of conversations as totally different **experiences**. How could that be?*

This is the thought that clicked in *my* head as I started listening to feedback from customers of the earliest companies to transform their service operations to DCS. These were the people who were among the first to experience OnScreen Enhancements seamlessly woven into their digital journeys.

I was thinking about all the data I've seen in the trade press over the past decade about "the increase in customer **resistance** to using the phone." The assumption has always been that as customers become more digitally self-sufficient, they don't want to have to *talk to anyone* any more.

For example, it's become conventional wisdom that *"millennials don't EVER talk on the phone – to anyone!"* So it makes sense that customer research shows increasing preference for texting over talking.

But here were these customers who were having their first-ever voice interactions with agents in DCS (through OnScreen Voice), and they were scoring 90 percent on CSAT, 15–20 points higher on NPS (and *lower* for customer effort) across the board. Older people *and* younger people.

So, if customers don't like talking to an agent, how could THAT be?

(continued)

What we're learning is: Customers don't, in fact, hate *talking*. What they hate is feeling forced to have to dial a phone number that is *disconnected from their digital experience*. Many will do almost anything to avoid having to.

But that can lead to other problems. What about situations that require additional diagnosis, or where a person isn't confident they know what they need or want? Those are handled much more effectively with a live interaction. Or what about situations in which an interaction with an agent could lead to *greater long-term revenue* for the company?

As we learn more about the psychology of customers who engage in DCS interactions, we're seeing that when a person is already in the midst of trying to do something on a website or app, if they need some help and have a verbal conversation with an agent through their screen – their reaction to that experience is almost 180-degrees different than if they had to give up and *then* dial a phone number.

The reason: In DCS, if you want to talk, there's no need to start all over. Whether it's an OnScreen Voice conversation or video chat, and especially if there's an opportunity for the customer and agent to be working on the same screen through CoBrowsing – it's still the *same two people*, taking care of the *same issue,* but it feels like a completely different *experience.*

People may not dislike "talking to another human being" as much as we've all been led to believe.

What they *really* dislike is having to stop what they were doing online, then finding a phone number, calling that number, going through a slew of IVR options (hoping they've picked the right selection) waiting on hold for who-knows-how-long, listening to the same looping soundtrack of elevator music (hoping they won't get disconnected) until an agent

(continued)

finally picks up . . . and THEN makes them start the process all over again.

Maybe that's the part they hate.

—DM

Let's reflect on of the benefits created by the transformation to a DCS service model – as experienced by *each* of the stakeholders in this "win-win-win-win" proposition.

WIN #1: THE BENEFITS OF DCS FOR COMPANIES

- Greater operational efficiency
- Increased online conversion rate
- Higher CSAT, NPS, and lower customer effort

In customer service, the battle between **cost** and **quality** has always been assumed to be a zero-sum equation – whatever you give to one side, must be taken from the other.

And in the analog world – the one in which customer service was built on a phone-first platform then got gussied-up with a few digital ornaments just to keep up with the times – at best, most companies attempt to *balance* the two outcomes. This can feel like an unending struggle.

But if a primary goal for any company is to acquire, retain and grow its customer base, the most significant benefit of a DCS service model is that it creates the ideal loyalty-boosting experience for customers, while also reducing operating costs.

That's like having your cake, eating it too, *and* losing weight in the process!

The First Hurdle: Calculating the Business Value of Transforming to DCS

No major initiative at any organization is likely to get the "green light" without the promise of a substantial ROI. And, as we will be sharing more stories from the companies that are already operating in a DCS environment throughout the book, we will be offering much of the ammunition you will need to make a compelling business case for digital transformation. But – for starters – here is the basic formula for determining the operational efficiency that can be achieved through this transformation:

- *Call data/cost.* Calculate the total number of minutes all agents are interacting with all customers by phone.
- *DCS opportunities.* Determine the percentage of incoming calls during which the customer is on or near a screen (smartphone, tablet, laptop, desktop). Every one of these interactions has high potential for improvement through DCS. Communication, automation, and collaboration can be introduced right on the customer's screen to make the experience far better (since they are already on the screen!).
  - Suggestion: Ask your agents, "How often are you getting calls to help a customer with something they are struggling to do online? How about something they could do online if you taught them how?"
- *DCS OnScreen benefits.* Calculate the cost savings and efficiency boost of using OnScreen communication, collaboration, and automation to:
- Decrease the handle time of each interaction.
- Enable customers to become more digitally self-sufficient, thus reducing their future dependence on live service.

EXAMPLE

Call data/cost: Imagine a company that receives one million phone calls annually, with an overall AHT (average handle time) of six minutes. That's six million minutes of talk time. Their annual staff budget is $3 million with a cost per minute of $0.50.

DCS opportunities: The percentage of customers who *could* have resolved their issue in self-service is about 50 percent. The percentage within that group of people who were near a screen at the moment of their call is 80 percent (remember, when a customer is calling from a smartphone they are already *on* a screen!)

This means about 40 percent of total annual call minutes could be influenced if they were transformed into a DCS experience. That's 2.4 million "influenceable minutes."

DCS OnScreen benefits: On average, a DCS interaction goes about one-third faster – because the customer and the agent are looking at the same exact thing, and the agent can show the customer where to find things on their own screen.

That's 800,000 minutes saved, or a savings of $400,000.

[And here comes the part where this formula starts to sound like a late-night infomercial . . . because . . . WAIT, there's still *more*!]

Now calculate the percentage of live phone minutes that could be eliminated with OnScreen Automation, situations in which bots could handle low-complexity issues and no live assistance is required. Most companies are reporting an average of about one out of five calls can be handled easily by bots – while still creating an excellent experience for the customer. That's another 1.2 million minutes (20 percent of the total 6M minutes of call time) that are no longer necessary, or a savings of $600,000.

$400k + $600k = $1,000,000 or one-third of the total staff budget now freed up.

And that's just "present ROI." One other future-looking consideration (a "glorious ancillary benefit") is the reduction of live phone volume going forward, as customers become more confident in their ability to resolve certain issues entirely in self-service. This could also lead to significant savings over time.

On average – companies that have transformed to DCS are realizing cost savings of at least 25–30 percent, while *also* increasing CSAT and NPS an average of 15–20 percent. That's the sweet spot. Any strategy that puts you at the intersection of operational efficiency *and* improved customer experience – is where you want to pitch your tent.

Preview of "DCS in Action" Stories

Throughout the book, we will share a number of stories based on the firsthand experiences of companies that are transforming their service operations to DCS. Here are a few highlights:

- *CoBrowsing creates major efficiency improvements.* We'll reveal the details of a company that has seen the mix of customers using phone-first vs. digital-first flip from 80/20 to 20/80 in the span of a year, greatly reducing their service costs.
- *DCS offers a differentiated service experience.* An organization discovers that seamless "DCS experiences" score as well (or better) for CSAT and NPS than live in-person interactions.
- *AI management makes agents more efficient.* With basic chores like authentication, issue diagnosis and accessing customer information all handled automatically by bots, average "agent time per interaction" at one organization was reduced by up to 5 minutes for some processes.

And while the cost of implementing DCS is based on vendor selection and other variables, it is substantially less than the savings most companies are achieving even in their first year of transformation.

WINNER = Company

WIN #2: THE BENEFITS OF DCS FOR CUSTOMERS

- Creates an experience that feels more like how customers live their lives
- Reduces customer effort in resolving service issues
- Enables affirmation of decision to choose your company

The Second Hurdle: Customers Expect Digital Experiences to Be Seamless and Perfect

Customer expectations for how service interactions should "feel" continue to evolve, seemingly faster than most companies can keep up with. But now there's a way for any company to meet and exceed these expectations.

Most people generally want four things from a service interaction:

1. Solve my problem so I don't have to think about it anymore.
2. Do it in a fast and easy way.
3. If possible, show *me* how to do it so I won't have to call again.
4. Make me feel smart for choosing your company.

Feedback from customers of companies that have transformed to a DCS service model say all four of these are generally accurate descriptions of *their* experiences.

To most customers, DCS experiences feel more like "personalized learning opportunities" than "service interactions." Plus, the interaction is taking place on *my* screen. Those differences completely change how customers feel about the quality of that experience.

Eliminating the Negative

One major source of high-effort service experiences is any situation in which a customer has to "switch channels" within one resolution journey. Most typically, that's when a customer starts online but at some point has to also call the company on the phone. In DCS, that never happens. Any transition between self-service, bot-assisted service and agent-assisted service occurs right on the customer's screen with no additional effort.

Making Me Feel Smart

One critical opportunity embedded within each service interaction is the opportunity to enable a customer to reaffirm their continued loyalty to that company. What we've learned over the years is that this future loyalty likely hinges on two considerations in the minds of customers:

- *Was that service interaction satisfactory?* Did I get resolution? Was the process relatively easy, or was it a nightmare to get what I wanted? Did it feel like the company was trying to help me, and make me feel like a valued customer, or did I feel like "just another number"?

This is the baseline of success for any interaction. But *here* is the opportunity:

- *Do I feel smarter as a result of this interaction?* Do I feel like the decision I made to choose this company was a good one, or am I thinking I could have done better for myself by going with a competitor? Do I feel like I understand something better as a result of this interaction? Did I learn anything of value?

Because many DCS OnScreen interactions are designed to *teach* customers (instead of just to "serve" them), there's a far greater likelihood that a customer will feel smarter as a result and therefore more loyal to that company.

DCS = Customer-Centricity

No customer (OK, the *tiniest* percentage) has any idea what customer service "system" a given company uses. Most people wouldn't know the difference between Cisco (the networking and telecoms company), Sysco (the restaurant supply company), and the Cisco Kid. *Don't know, don't care.*

But when there's a problem or issue that needs to be dealt with, what customers *do* care about is how they feel about the way your company is handling it.

Take care of *me. I* am the customer – I've chosen to do business with you (and I have more choices than ever before!) When there's a problem – serve me where *I live* – on my own screen.

In today's customer environment, DCS is the embodiment of **customer-centricity**.

WINNER = Customers.

WIN #3: THE BENEFITS OF DCS FOR AGENTS

- Elevation of reputation and impact on company success
- Increased employee engagement
- Greater job satisfaction

The Third Hurdle: Getting Your Frontline Team on Board

While the first consideration in any transformation must always be the economics and ROI, at least some mindshare needs to be paid to the potential impact on employee engagement, job satisfaction, performance, turnover, and overall morale.

Most DCS companies are reporting that this has turned out to be the easiest of all the perceived hurdles to overcome. Once agents understand how this transformation will make their jobs way easier, it will not be a hard sell. Being an agent in this digitally transformed environment has changed the role of frontline employees from being "customer service reps" to becoming DCS "superagents."

Even among long-tenured reps, the image of the role they are playing in the organization is, itself transforming. What was once a "production job" or perhaps an "information worker" becomes the role of "teacher and enabler of digital proficiency among our customers."

The job itself is less about *serving people*. It's about being an *expert who represents customers, and helps them feel smarter about themselves.*

When this updated role imagery is combined with the addition of new agent-assistant automation (which eliminates the need for verbal authentication, issue identification, customer information – which are all done before the agent enters the discussion), the frontline job becomes easier, more satisfying, and in many cases more fun.

The Impact on Staffing Levels/Headcount

Over time, a typical DCS operation will likely require fewer agents as greater efficiency is achieved through OnScreen Enhancements. This reduction could be resolved through downsizing, but most organizations experience enough frontline turnover that headcount reductions can often be accomplished through attrition.

The message to your frontline needs to become crystal clear:

Yes, over time we will likely need fewer total people in our service operation than in the past, and this newer job isn't going to be right for everyone. For those of you who choose to remain and adapt to DCS, the image and impact of what you do will increase over time. The job will become different, but different in a better way.

DCS isn't about "the robots taking our jobs," it's about "letting the bots do what bots do best" so that we people can "do what humans do best."

Some companies are even choosing to redeploy a percentage of the cost savings achieved through lower call volume to escalate the pay rates of agents who excel in a DCS environment. How does that sound?

WINNER = Agents and Service Team

WIN #4: THE BENEFITS OF DCS FOR SERVICE EXECUTIVES AND LEADERS

- Simplified operational management
- Higher staff performance, ability to recruit higher-quality candidates
- Positive impact on career trajectory

The Final Hurdle: What's in It for Me?

Asking this question might feel selfish at some level. Because if there is a new strategy or solution that will help your company, as well as your customers and your team – well, those should be reasons enough for you to be moved to action, right?

But (c'mon!) don't we always factor any decision or strategy around the question: "How is this going to benefit *me*?"

And, like the other hurdles, this one is also close to a no-brainer. Based on the experiences of those service leaders who are further down the road of digital transformation, creating a lower-effort digital experience for customers is also lower-effort for leaders, managers, and supervisors.

Because DCS creates a "channelless" experience, there is no need to manage separate teams – one for chat, one for phone, one for text/social, etc. You are managing an entire team of "superagents." As such, you will begin to attract and retain better talent. The greater the job satisfaction, the easier it is to manage people.

Smarter Analytics = Easier Improvement Opportunities

DCS creates a natural opportunity to build a bridge between the service team and the digital team. Because analytics are now gathered within a single engagement format (instead of separately by interaction type) most companies discover that they can spot efficiency opportunities earlier. By learning the exact moments within a given process or interaction where customers are likely to need assistance, bots can be quickly adjusted to intervene before the customer even realizes they need help.

Plus, with agent-assistant bots proactively offering suggested next steps to the frontline and providing instant solutions for customer issues, reliance on supervisors will decrease correspondingly. Imagine if the role of supervisor were to transform into becoming a true mentor role instead of being a glorified tier II agent.

Consider Your Next Performance Review

Instead of constantly being in *firefighting mode,* leaders in a DCS environment are enabled to use design thinking to develop continuous improvements in digital customer journeys. This is not only more interesting and satisfying work, but you're helping to accomplish two of your company's most important goals simultaneously – greater operational efficiency *and* greater customer loyalty.

The next time you sit down with your supervisor (or if you're CEO, the next time the board reviews your performance), how would you feel if you came armed with a deck showing you've found a way to accomplish *that*?

WINNER = Leaders

CUSTOMERS HAVE TRANSFORMED; SO SHOULD YOUR COMPANY

The assumed solution to overcoming the challenges of creating an excellent experience for increasingly empowered (and in some cases *entitled*) digital customers has been: Companies must "meet their customers where they are."

This has generally been interpreted as "meet them in the **channel** where they started their interaction."

And of course, most likely that is *not* the phone anymore – but rather, your website, mobile app, or social media sites like Facebook and Twitter – so the conventional wisdom is that you need to meet them *there*. And while this seems correct, we are learning that it is an *underintrepretation* of the concept.

To successfully transform customer service in a digital world, companies must "meet their customers where they are" in two *other* ways as well:

■ *Meet them where they are at a specific moment in a resolution journey.* By the time a customer speaks with an agent, that customer has already been through some form of misadventure that very likely began online. Companies can no longer greet customers at the outset of a phone interaction like it's *the starting point* for that person's service journey, because it almost certainly isn't.

Where they *are* – is in the middle of their *digital experience.*

■ *Meet them where they are in their digital lifestyles.* Most customers now instinctively reach for their smartphone, tablet, or laptop as *the* starting point for interactions of all kinds as well as to satisfy their information, entertainment, and recreation needs. Companies need to create service experiences that feel like the way their customers now live.

Where they *are* – is in the middle of their own *digital transformation*.

Your ability to meet your customers where they are in *all three ways* should become the beacon for the digital transformation of your service organization.

As much as customer behavior has been transforming over the past decade, the underlying psychology and sociology that drives those behaviors has been changing even faster. What we've been learning is that the more you understand and appreciate *why* this is happening, the easier it will be for you to create a strategy that can meet and exceed ever-escalating customer expectations in the digital world.

Here's a preview of what you can expect in the chapters to follow:

- In **Chapters 2 and 3** we will explore the evolution of service over the past decade, and the corresponding evolution of customer expectations and psychology.
  - Why do so many customers have a negative bias against customer service, how does that impact their online behaviors – and what can companies do to overcome this negative predisposition?
  - How did the advent of self-service lead to the unexpected consequence of setting a course of an ever-increasing demand for more and better digital experiences
    - By understanding *why* customer psychology and behaviors have been transforming, it becomes that much more clear why *you* have to transform.

- **Chapter 4** provides us with a common language and vocabulary for understanding the benefits of transforming to DCS. The integration of OnScreen Communication, OnScreen Collaboration, and OnScreen Automation in the DCS platform will be described in full detail.
- **Chapters 5–7** are a step-by-step guide for how to move away from a service-operation-centered phone interactions that are disconnected from the digital experience – by focusing on three strategic areas:
  - *Process* – how to get started with DCS and accelerate your progress
  - *People* – how DCS changes the way your people work, and the satisfaction they get from their jobs
  - *Positioning* – how DCS gives your company a competitive advantage and positions service as a true differentiator

KEY TAKEAWAYS: CHAPTER 1

- *Everyone comes out a winner.* The transformation to DCS creates benefits for all – for companies, their customers, their service teams, and those who lead them.

- *Don't focus on channels; the goal is seamlessness.* DCS isn't about adding new digital channels to service, it's about creating digital customer journeys that move customers from self-service to agent-assistance in ways that are seamless and effortless for both the customer and the agent.

- *You must meet your customers where they are (x3!).* While DCS enables customers to contact a company any way they like, it also meets them in two other ways: in the middle of the journey they have already started, and within their own personal transformation to living in an on-screen world.

CHAPTER 2

The Peaks and Valleys of Customer Service

What we'll share in this chapter:

- Call centers (and the toll-free numbers companies offer) were once a value-add for customers, and the quality of the phone experience was of paramount importance to most companies.

- But over time, the fundamental corporate desire to constantly drive down operating expenses set up a tug-of-war between **cost** and **quality** in service. It was no contest.

- Amplified by an inherently negative societal bias, the **reputation** of customer service declined.

- However, the source of this negativity has evolved over time – from frustration over phone experiences, to frustrations experienced during digital interactions. And while this changing dynamic creates a different challenge, it is considerably easier to overcome.

"Yeah, Phil, I just wanna warn you, I'm really frustrated so I'm probably gonna ruin your Average Handle Time for the day."

IT WASN'T ALWAYS THIS WAY

If you're under the age of about 55 or so, it might be hard to imagine that there was a time when call centers were considered a "bonus" for customers. It's true.

The option to reach customer service by phone hadn't existed previously, other than to call a corporate switchboard (with 25 people sitting in front of a wall of crisscrossed wires), hoping to reach someone in the Complaint Department.

And while some companies had been operating outbound "boiler room" sales centers – the first one, Dial America, was created by Time Inc. in 1957 to hustle subscriptions to *Life* magazine – the term *call center* was only first recognized by the *Oxford English Dictionary* in 1983. That's the year when the now-defunct trade magazine *Data Communications* ran the first-known feature article describing the operations of customer service taking place in a call center setting.

And if you're younger than about 45 or so, it might be hard to imagine that there was a time when being able to reach the Customer Service Department using a "toll-free" telephone number made it feel like you were getting away with something. Almost like stealing. And as more companies expanded their calling hours – some were even available on weekends! – customers and companies both agreed: We've got a hit on our hands!

> When companies started touting that "you can now call directly and be connected with a customer service expert any time you like," that was a real differentiator. For a time.

But over the past few decades the general reputation of "customer service call centers" has transformed. Here's a composite of how the service experience is typically described in customer focus groups:

From the moment you're confronted with a menu of choices in a "phone tree" narrated by some robo-voice ("for billing issues please press *7 . . .") you already know that whatever you choose is going to be "just the starting point" in an unguided and meandering journey in quest of getting SOMEONE to help you solve your problem.

What happens from there . . . could be . . . anything. There's no telling how many times you'll have to explain or re-explain your issue. There's no telling if the person you end up talking to will understand your issue . . . or even your words. There's no telling how long this might take, or if you'll ever get whatever the heck it is you need.

What was once a true "difference maker in customer experience" has now been relegated to being just another pain-in-the-butt on your to-do list.

What happened? And who's to blame?

Story: The Billboard

It wasn't just a bad day, but the worst kind of day for anyone who's ever worked in a call center. A Monday morning, and the queue was slammed and jammed from the moment Justin Robbins came out of the elevator. He was early, arriving a few minutes before 8. A Wawa coffee still steamed in his hand.

Justin was working at the Hershey Resorts contact center, and although he was only in his late twenties, he'd already been "in the game" for more than a decade. He got his first taste of customer service at age 12 working as a paperboy for the Press-Enterprise in Bloomsburg, Pennsylvania. He and a few other newsies were offered a few bucks an hour to cold-call local residents to sell more subscriptions. After the first few days, he was hooked.

It was a big step up to represent such a well-respected brand as Hershey and its three resorts.

The theme park is excellent and the tours are fun, but if you've never been to Hershey, Pennsylvania, you might not be aware that the hospitality is absolutely top-notch as well. Their flagship property, the Hotel Hershey, is as lovely as elegant old hotels get, with the aroma of warm chocolate filling the place day and night.

Justin had worked his way up from the floor to become a supervisor – but on *that* day – instead of heading into his new office – he immediately grabbed a headset, found a vacant workstation, plugged in, and helped the team siphon off the overflow in the steadily mounting queue.

(continued)

He got a quick briefing on the situation – the customer service team had apparently been "blindsided" by the marketing department, which had launched a big promotion that day. Apparently, they forgot to close the loop with the service team to let them know it was coming. Oops.

It was one of those "kids stay/play/eat free" campaigns that family resorts like to drop into the calendar to fill out the shoulder season. But it was loaded with exceptions and disclaimers and blackout dates that weren't quite clearly spelled out in that big ad on the front page of *USA Today*. Oops.

Many customers had to be told that, ". . . sorry . . . your preferred dates are blocked . . . and the food credit is limited to only certain outlets . . . and not all the properties were available on all dates . . ." People were pissed off.

After many hours of trying to "create a consistently excellent experience," the shift finally ended and Justin bolted out the double doors at the bottom of the service stairs to go for a long drive to decompress.

It was a lovely early spring afternoon. He aimed his sights down Route 322, a tranquil byway along the banks of the Susquehanna, set amidst the mountainous backdrop of the Tuscarora State Forest.

But just as his breathing was normalizing and his blood pressure was starting to recede, *he saw it* – off to the right, nestled in a grove of oak trees – a billboard for a local insurance agency, with a message that hit him like a harpoon in the chest:

We don't have call centers. We have <u>quality</u> service.

Imagine that. Taking a potshot at an entire profession. MY profession. And not only that it's OK to do it, but it's now become a marketing hook!

(continued)

That was the moment that triggered everything that would happen in Justin's career from that point forward. "In people's minds, they've dehumanized our profession. They now think of having to call customer service as this undesirable, horrible thing you want to avoid at all costs. It's a matter of perception and reality . . . and the *reality* is that the *perception* of what we do sucks."

Instead of quitting and never coming back to the call center ever again (a logical choice), or jerking the wheel hard to the right to knock the legs out from under that damned billboard (a dramatic choice), he decided on a more *thoughtful* choice – to try to understand *why* such a message would resonate with so many people and how the profession he loved so well had gotten to the point where it was regularly being mocked and ridiculed.

He is now the chief evangelist for CX Effect – a consultancy that offers strategic support to heads of customer experience – helping companies overcome the negative impact of this well-ingrained bias.

HOW DID CUSTOMER SERVICE BECOME SUCH AN EASY "PUNCHING BAG?"

Here's a question that doesn't feel good to have to ask, but it's worth thinking about (or at least having a good self-effacing laugh over – just among ourselves!): How does it feel to be part of a profession that is generally regarded so negatively by people? To be part of a profession that – if we're being honest – is an easy one for people to beat up on?

If there was a question on the TV game show *Family Feud* like: **"Name a job where a lot of people are angry at you,"** one could imagine Steve Harvey saying:

"Show me . . . customer service . . . (ding ding ding) . . . It's Number 3 on the board."

(By the way, Number 1 is: IRS agent)

Now, for a lot of service executives and leaders, the first natural reaction to this negative bias would likely be defensive: "Yeah, but service has improved GREATLY in the past decade. We've made so much progress with new channels and new technologies and new ways to engage our customers. As a collective discipline, we in service are way better than we used to be. That's a fact."

And of course that's true. There's no question among anyone in the research or analytics community that the general level of service being provided by companies has significantly improved over the past few years (and can now be measured every minute of every day – for quality assurance!).

So . . . *who's* to blame for this inherent, ingrained negative bias against "customer service?" You can't blame customers – that's just how they're wired.

CUSTOMERS ARE WIRED FOR NEGATIVE REACTIONS

To understand why humans would have a negative predisposition toward any specific experience (like calling customer service) might seem like an emotional consideration. But in this case – whether it's untrue or at least somewhat outdated – this bias is not, in fact, an *emotional* reaction. It is entirely *rational* and explainable based on two factors:

1. *Customer baggage*[1]. This is the more obvious factor. The perception of "customer service" isn't based solely on experiences people are having with your company, but to some extent by negative interactions they've had with *all* companies.
2. *Stickiness*. The lesser-considered factor is the impact of customer emotions during service interactions. Experiences that trigger a negative emotional reaction are inherently more memorable.

Roger Paulson is one of the few customer service authorities who doesn't work for a company – he resides in the academic world. For the past 15 years, he has served as customer service practice director at the University of Wisconsin's E-Business Consortium – a collaborative learning community and membership organization open to leaders of customer service and customer experience – the only of its kind affiliated with a major university.

He says:

It starts from a recognition of the fact that even in the best of cases, these kinds of service interactions are conceived with negative karma. People don't want to have to interact with customer service. All of the different ways we have to spend our time just makes us feel busier and a service interaction is an interruption that no one wants. Plus there's the hassle factor—whether real or imagined, the perception is that it's not going to be quick or easy.

There's this sense that I've purchased something, and yet I'm having an issue, and now you've interrupted my life, so now I can't enjoy the thing I've purchased. It's basic psychology. We're wired to remember when our hand gets burned on the stove, not when we put on a pair of warm mittens on a cold day.

Author and speaker Ty Bennett agrees, and then some. He has written four books on leadership and communication strategies and is well-known for his keynote presentation "The Psychology of Customer Service":

The human brain is engineered to overweight negative experiences five times more than positive experiences, and this has been borne out in experiments that analyze our brain's chemistry in a variety of different situations. We've been built that way to avoid pain and stay safe. So what happens with customer service is that bad experiences tend to create more memorable, tellable stories that are more likely to spread. It only makes sense that the negative ones would move faster and be more impactful.

The Story We've All Heard a Million Times

For a moment, separate yourself from your professional responsibilities and think about family celebrations and gatherings you've been to throughout your life. Once the beverages start to flow and the conversation gets a little more animated, isn't there always someone (it might be Uncle Somebody-or-other, holding court in the kitchen) launching into a long-winded tirade about an issue they had with some company?

A billing mix-up, a botched repair, a run-in, or dispute of some kind.

These stories are so ubiquitous that we've all heard versions of them a million times. And there's a reason why. The commonality of these negative experiences has become something like a shared language. They are easy fodder.

When people tell each other stories about negative service experiences, there's a pretty good chance someone else will jump in and try to top the last person's story. "Oh yeah, that same thing happened to me, only *worse!*"

The societal negativity around service experiences is so pervasive, it's been the subject of an ongoing study that started in the bicentennial year of 1976 in Washington, DC, when the White House Office of Consumer Affairs launched the first-ever **National Customer Rage Study.**

Initiated by US Attorney General Elliott Richardson (who served in the cabinets of both Richard Nixon and Gerald Ford), the first iteration of the study was produced by a team of Harvard University students who were assigned to explore how companies handle complaints.

And despite all the changes and updates to the service models of most companies over the decades since, the most recent Rage Study (in 2020) showed a continual decline in the overall reputation of customer service:

- The percentage of American consumers who say they have experienced a significant *problem* with a company they do business with continues to increase:
  - 32 percent in 1976
  - 42 percent in 2013
  - 66 percent in 2020
- Two-thirds of customers who have a problem will experience some form of "rage," triggered by having to expend

considerable effort to get their issue resolved, and a corresponding lack of confidence they will receive anything in return.

- Poor customer service experiences now put an estimated $494 billion in revenue at risk for American companies.[2]

Whether you like it or not, whether you wish it wasn't true – if you are in any position to influence the long-term loyalty of your customers – you might as well accept that most people are way more likely to engage in any service interaction *starting* with a negative mindset.

This appears to be a virtual certainty that has been driven into our brains, now lodged near where Instinct Blvd. picks up the Societally Reinforced Freeway.

Probably no one has studied the evolution of customer service more than Brad Cleveland. He was one of the original partners in ICMI – the International Customer Management Institute – established in the late 1980s; Brad served as CEO and president for 11 years. He says, "Somewhere down through the layers of how we're processing all this . . . I don't think we put enough thought into the psychological part of customer expectations. Someday we'll look back and wonder why we didn't put more thought into how all this is impacting us."

So . . . when it comes to the negative societal bias most people carry around against customer service, we can't blame customers. That's just how they're wired.

Then . . . who *can* we blame? We can't blame companies, either. That's just how *they're* wired.

COMPANIES ARE WIRED FOR EFFICIENCY

It's always been hard for most companies to commit significant resources against how service interactions "feel" at a subjective, psychological level, when it is so much more logical to base decisions on cost efficiency and immediate ROI.

There's a name for that – it's called **business**.

Among C-suite executives, the generally accepted mental model is that service is a "cost center" – an "unavoidable cost of doing business." Taken from an economic standpoint, it might seem to make sense to do everything possible to reduce the cost to serve customers. If you were to think like a CFO – with a strictly logical Vulcan mindset – what other conclusion could you reach?

Once we've made a sale, that's all the money we're going to make from that transaction. Sure there are all kinds of long-term considerations that fit into the realm of "customer loyalty" but those may only bear fruit at some undefined future date.

For right now, we've received X-amount from X-customer, and we realized X-profit, but what remains unknown is how much it will cost to serve that customer. And that's unsettling, because customer service is expensive.

Customer service industry analyst Blair Pleasant of COMMfusion says she's observed a kind of myopia among senior executives: "Yes, there are some companies that do service right, but way more companies that don't. They look at customer service as something they have to do, and they want to do it as cheaply as possible and it doesn't feel like it's their top priority. I think a lot of them understand the importance of customer loyalty and customer satisfaction, but for many of them it's just more about the constant pressure to cut costs, and because there are so many people involved, contact centers are considered expensive."

Customer service does cost a lot. A 2019 report in *Harvard Business Review* estimated that the price tag for serving customers and solving problems – after they'd already purchased – cost companies more than $38 billion.[3]

So, as an efficiency play, many service leaders started focusing more scrutiny on their employees to cut customer calls as short as possible by reducing AHT (average handle time). But that only tended to make the agent's job harder, which had a downstream impact on employee turnover, and certainly didn't improve the customer experience in any way.

COST EATS QUALITY FOR LUNCH

Sure, every company says they want to do what's right – for customers *and* the bottom line. But the lure of cost-optimization became more and more powerful around the time of the millennium. And as most of us have observed in our careers, any time push comes to shove, the scale invariably ends up tipping to the financial side of the equilibrium.

Perhaps no other single stage in the evolution of customer service fueled the fire of public negativity more than the outsourcing boom of the late 1990s and early 2000s. During that time, it felt to many customers like every company was suddenly shifting the responsibility of interacting with customers to agents who seemed to be working out of "overseas" call centers.

It is estimated that in less than a decade, over a quarter-million call center jobs were outsourced from the US to a range of other countries – including the Philippines and India, among others.[4]

EXAMPLE

At that time, the national estimate of the all-in costs for a US call center employee (including benefits and other fixed costs) was somewhere between $22 and $35 per hour. That same person-hour contracted through an outsourcing vendor might cost between $8 and $14 in the Philippines, and as low as $5 to $9 in India.[5]

To many CEOs and CFOs, it seemed like a no-brainer. But it became *no bargain*.

Cultural and language barriers were often major issues, the telephony was wonky, environmental noise was a distraction that hindered clear communication – all of which created a suboptimal customer experience. This was further amplified in outsourcing call centers where employee morale was low due to poor working conditions.

Even to customers who had little or no understanding of the customer service business, it became increasingly obvious that in "the horse race between cost and quality," cost was leading by a comfortable five lengths as they headed around the clubhouse turn.

This only served to exacerbate the growing negative perception of the customer service industry as a whole.

The mounting backlash against outsourcing and the result-ing job losses became so pervasive that Congress was called on to do something about it. One of a number of bills was introduced under the umbrella heading of the United States Call Center Worker and Consumer Protection Act, requiring businesses that employ 50 or more employees to notify the Department of Labor at least 120 days before relocating such centers outside of the United States. Civil penalties of up to $10,000 a day were pro-posed, as well as directing the Secretary of Labor to maintain and make publicly available a list of all such employers that relocate a call center.[6]

Adding to the frustration for customers, "When there's an issue of some kind, there's a fundamental mismatch of serious-ness levels," says Ty Bennett. "When I have a problem it's a one-time event for me, cause I'm the only one here and it's happening to me. But to someone working in a call center (especially in an outsourcing model), if you're the 999-thousandth customer with that same exact problem, it's very easy for an agent to become bored doing the same thing over and over. Customer expecta-tions are always increasing, and yet companies are incentivizing the wrong activities: speed, efficiency, and volume."

If the general reputation of customer service wasn't already bad enough, the pressure to continue cutting costs – epitomized by the outsourcing boom – sent it plummeting to even greater depths.

So, *who's* to blame for this pervasive negative perception that has an impact on EVERY interaction you have every day with your customers?

- *You can't blame **customers***. Most people have accumulated a wealth of negative experiences with customer service over time that are then amplified by our inherent human psychol-ogy and their viral nature.

- *You can't blame **companies**.* Businesses must always focus on efficiency – so, reducing handle times and moving to outsourcing felt like necessities in order to stay competitive.

EVOLUTION OF CUSTOMER SERVICE: THE "QUALITY VALLEY"

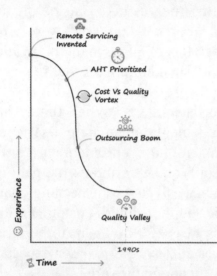

When live phone customer service was first introduced, customers were impressed by being able to speak to an "expert," with a toll-free call no less! At that time, the strategic emphasis for most companies was on the *quality* of the service experience, which was generally high.

However, the corporate imperative to constantly drive down costs led to *competing priorities* between service and the C-suite. Many companies increased the pressure on their service agents to shorten the duration of customer interactions (AHT), and then came the outsourcing boom. The combined effect of this "cost vs. quality" vortex sent the overall reputation of customer service careening toward rock-bottom.

So . . . what to do? One can imagine the hushed conversation in corporate boardrooms, at executive retreats, and around customer service conference tables:

OK, call centers are people-intensive and expensive – a live interaction with a customer ties up one employee for however long as that call takes. One customer, one agent.

Not scalable.

*But . . . finding the cheapest labor in the world to handle service issues . . . or pressuring our reps to keep their calls as short as possible . . . is that **really** what we want to do?*

*Think about it: If there's only one person representing our company in each interaction, don't we want that person to be someone we're proud to have on the front line greeting our customers? Someone you'd be proud for your Mom to talk to? **Sounds great, but sounds expensive.***

But what if there was another way to cut costs? What if there was a way to enable customers to "serve themselves?"

*That would solve the **cost** problem . . . and if the experience was acceptable . . . it might even solve the **quality** problem as well. Bingo!*

What could possibly go wrong?

KEY TAKEAWAYS: CHAPTER 2

- *You're already starting behind the 8-ball.* The inherently negative perception of customer service may not be fair, but it's reality. Humans are conditioned to remember negative experiences more than positive ones, and many service issues are driven by a problem or issue a customer didn't want to deal with in the first place. If the whole thing is perceived as a big hassle, that only imprints the experience more deeply.

- *Cost of service vs. quality of experience is not exactly a fair fight.* While no company would ever say, "We're OK with our customers having poor experiences," the instinct to reduce operating costs is almost irresistible.

- *Customers have been sucked into a vortex of negativity.* The more that businesses worked to squeeze efficiency out of their service operations, the more negative experiences were created for customers. This downward spiral led to a continual decline in customer experience and reinforced the negative perception of call center operations.

CHAPTER 3

Digital Self-Service Changed Things Forever

What we'll share in this chapter:

- Customer self-service was introduced in the late 1970s, and at first, companies had to work hard to achieve "adoption" of these new technologies.

- Eventually, customers not only got used to the idea of serving themselves but became "hooked" and started demanding more and more.

- Many companies found themselves in a race against ever-increasing customer expectations for greatly improved digital interactions.

- What started as a cost-optimization play became a classic case of "be careful what you wish for."

"How come if Facebook knows I'm on JCPenney,
JCPenney doesn't know I'm on JCPenney?"

THE CITI NEVER SLEEPS

Every digital self-service interaction you've experienced in your lifetime can be traced back to a single event.

Actually, it was two events: The Blizzards of 1978 – a pair of ripsaw Nor'easters that swept up the Atlantic coast that winter – one in January and the other right on its heels in February.

In New York City, facing days of snowbound paralysis with streets blocked off by massive drifts, tens of thousands of people engaged in an activity they had never done before: Getting cash from a machine, instead of from a live teller.

Self-service was born.

The ATM was originally conceived by British inventor John Shepherd-Brown, who (according to legend) was neck-deep in a bubble bath when he came up with a crazy idea: If a vending machine could dispense candy bars, why couldn't we come up with one that spit out cash, instead of 3 Musketeers?

The mechanics of the prototype weren't hard to figure out, but it was only when he joined forces with Scottish engineer James Goodfellow that self-service technology was considered viable. Goodfellow had come up with the missing piece of the puzzle – the Personal Identification Number (PIN) system that allowed electronic banking transactions to become secure.[1]

Citibank was among the first financial institutions to take the leap and start purchasing automated teller machines, branded as Citicard Banking Centers (CBCs). In late 1977, after conducting user testing and several rounds of market studies, the company spent over $100 million to install ATMs in all five New York boroughs.

To say that the launch went over like a lead balloon would be an insult to the fine people in the lead industry.

Despite the positive response from focus group subjects in sterile research settings, the vast majority of everyday customers couldn't quite warm up to the idea of conducting financial transactions via a vending machine.

For almost two centuries, banking in the United States had always meant going into a branch, filling out a form using the pen-on-a-chain, waiting in a snaking velour-roped line and speaking with a human teller. Giving some newfangled machine complete access to your bank account – without any way of knowing whether it was truly secure – was *scary*.

And if getting cash *out* of a Citibank Banking Center wasn't daunting enough, the idea of depositing cash or a check *into* a robo-teller was out of the question entirely.

But then the blizzards hit. The first one left the city buried under nearly 20 inches of snow, and the second one almost as much. Banks were closed for days, and the only way people could access their money was through the new CBCs.

Usage increased over 20 percent during the first storm, and another 20 percent during the second.[2]

Word spread fast:

Why wait in a long teller line when you can just walk up and serve yourself? Why be worried about someone looting your account as long as you're the only one who knows your PIN code? It's faster, it's easier, it's just as safe and it puts you in total control over your money – which you can now access any time, any day.

Citibank thus became the first-ever 24/7 financial institution. Their marketing team seized on this singular point of differentiation by creating a tag-line that served them well for years:

The Citi Never Sleeps.[3]

FROM MIGRATION TO EXPECTATION TO DEMAND

Although it started strictly as a cost-cutting move ("If we could somehow get customers to do basic transactions *themselves,* imagine how much we could save!"), self-service transformed from something customers were willing to tolerate, to one they began to appreciate, to one they now expect and *demand*.

If you were to picture a classic "evolution chart," the self-service version would look like this[4]:

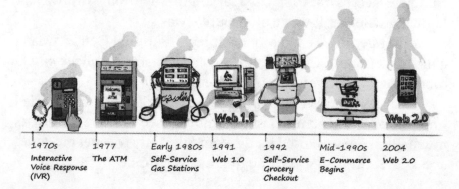

1970s	1977	Early 1980s	1991	1992	Mid-1990s	2004
Interactive Voice Response (IVR)	The ATM	Self-Service Gas Stations	Web 1.0	Self-Service Grocery Checkout	E-Commerce Begins	Web 2.0

1970s: Interactive Voice Response

As customer service matured, new innovations followed. One of the earliest breakthroughs was interactive voice response. IVR paved the way for substantial improvements in nonhuman automated service *(to repeat this description, please press "4").*

1977: The ATM

Thank you, Mr.'s Shepherd-Brown and Goodfellow, for inventing it!

Early 1980s: Self-Service Gas Stations

Frank Ulrich invented the self-service gas station in 1947. But pay-at-the-pump didn't come along until the mid-1970s, and shortly after that, self-service stations became rule rather than the exception. *Except* in Oregon and New Jersey, where – to this day – all gas pumps are still operated by attendants.

> *NOTE: Growing up in Virginia, my son had never been to a full-service gas station in his life and didn't even know there was such a thing. During a road trip when he was about nine years old we stopped in New Jersey for a fill-up. Looking out the window from the back seat, he panicked for a moment, "Dad, what is that man DOING?"*
>
> *"Don't worry, son, that's what gas stations used to be like in the olden days."*
>
> *—RD*

1991: Web 1.0

The initial launch of the World Wide Web was based entirely on providing access to static sites that displayed basic information with little interactive capability. But at the time, it was still considered miraculous – like having full access to everything in the Library of Congress while sitting at your kitchen table in a bathrobe!

1992: Self-Service Grocery Checkout Stations

The first grocery store to feature "service robots" (as they were called at the time) was a Price Chopper in Clifton Park, New York. *Price check on Robot 3, please.*

Mid-1990s: E-commerce Begins

Amazon launched in July 1995 as an online bookstore, but didn't report its first annual profit until 2003. *Mr. Bezos's eight-year wait to get into the black seems to have paid off. Ya think?*

2004: Web 2.0

Coined by Irish technology visionary Tim O'Reilly at the O'Reilly Media Web Conference in San Francisco, the "re-birth" of the internet was designed around ease of use, democratization of content creation, participatory culture, and interoperability.

It was Web 2.0 that changed everything in self-service. Processes that were once only available offline were now online. Functionality that was once only accessible to agents inside the four walls of a company via back-end systems (ordering, booking, account maintenance) were now – for the first time ever – open and available for use by customers themselves. On their *own screens.*

Before long, as adoption and utilization of self-service sky-rocketed, *the screen* became the center of the universe for most people. Today, customers are more likely to leave you if you *don't* let them serve themselves.

From reluctance . . . to acceptance . . . to expectation . . . to demand. The evolution has now reached its final destination.

NEVER GOING BACK AGAIN

Why exactly did self-service start to exert such a powerful hold on customers and their behavior? The answer is based on two considerations – one logical, the other emotional – **convenience** and **agency**.

Shep Hyken is considered one of the world's most prolific thought leaders in the customer service space. He is the author of seven books, has performed over 500 keynote addresses at industry and association conferences, and is the recipient of a Lifetime Achievement Award from the National Speakers Association Hall of Fame.

In his book *The Convenience Revolution*,[5] Shep says the ever-increasing public appetite for self-service experiences was inevitable once people got their first taste:

> *When the airlines first came out with online reservations for simple bookings, the premise was to allow their live phone agents to focus on more complex and profitable interactions. And in order to entice first-timers, many of them offered promotions to customers, saying, "If you book online, we'll give you a bonus" . . . and from there, most of us would never think of calling to purchase a ticket ever again.*
>
> *Same thing with online boarding passes. Why would you EVER print out a boarding pass when it's already in*

your phone? That's not an extra service anymore, it's an expectation – for some customers it feels like it's their right to be able to serve themselves.

Being in control over being able to get what you want, when you want it, the way you want it, is a powerful influence on customer behavior.

And if **convenience** explains the outsized demand for self-service at a more *logical* level, it is **agency** that completes the explanation at a more *emotional* level.

In their book *The Power of Agency*,[6] Paul Napper and Anthony Rao describe the psychological power of the human need for control:

Agency is what allows you to pause, evaluate, and act when you face a challenge—be it at work, home, or anywhere else in the world. Agency is about being active rather than passive, of reacting effectively to immediate situations and planning effectively for your future. In simpler words, agency is what humans have always used to feel in command of their lives.

Maybe self-service is less about "service" and more about "self."

Story: Three Sad Faces

Have you ever stayed in a hotel that is one of the Grand Dames of its city? The classics. There are a few that come to mind: The Plaza in New York, The Hay-Adams in DC, The Fontainebleau in Miami Beach, The Peabody in Memphis (you know, the one with the ducks). Iconic hotels.

(continued)

But about a decade ago, the "classics" started to run into a problem – they all had to be "digitally updated." Yes, it is glorious to check into your elegant room at some historic gem of a property, but it's a bit of a buzzkill when you realize there's no USB port anywhere near the bed. *Raise your hand if you've ever had to unplug a hotel lamp to find an outlet for your laptop charger.* Some hotel companies were quicker than others to pick up on the impact of digital transformation on customer loyalty.

The Hilton Chicago fits the classic hotel motif to a "T." Situated oh-so-perfectly on The Miracle Mile across the street from Grant Park, its very location defines Chicago. The hotel proudly boasts that every US president since 1927 has spent at least a night there. And because it's such an amazing hotel, I expected the lobby to be packed when I was checking in one fall afternoon, but at that moment there was absolutely *nobody* in front of me. *Jackpot!*

I've always hated waiting in lines, and it feels like a bonus when you don't *have to* – especially in high-traffic areas like airport security, the men's room during the seventh-inning stretch at a baseball game, or a big hotel lobby.

There were three check-in positions open that afternoon, with three crisply attired agents at the ready to create a warm Platinum welcome. As I approached from the back of the lobby, I briefly wondered whether one of them would declare they were "it," and that I should come to their station. Or, whether I'd have to make the choice myself (then awkwardly explain during the check-in banter why I picked *them* – which I'm sure would have been chuckled at, courteously).

(continued)

But as I got most of the way to the desk, I was halted by the sight of a brand new digital offering at the Hilton – apparently just introduced that month – two side-by-side self-service check-in kiosks.

In an awkward move that felt less like a choice, and more like an instinct, I heel-turned 90-degrees to the right and started in without a thought – touching the screen, sticking in my corporate Amex and activating my session.

And THAT was the moment I realized:

I am now permanently "wired" to prefer, expect, and demand self-service.

I love being able to take care of business *myself*. It's easy. And I'm the kind of person who has always taken joy out of "skipping the line" whenever possible.

But what I learned on that day . . . is that it was never about *the line*. Because there was no line.

It's just that the "freedom" of self-service now has such a powerful hold on me that if the option is available, I'm taking it. Every time. And the number of people who feel the same way increases every year. Especially now that we've all experienced what it's like to serve ourselves through a pandemic.

I can still picture their three sad faces, shoulders slumped in resignation that I chose zero of them. As I was walking toward the elevators with my room key freshly delivered by the kiosk, I momentarily thought about walking back to the check-in desk and apologizing.

Now I'm sorry I didn't.

—RD

EVOLUTION OF CUSTOMER SERVICE: THE DIGITAL SELF-SERVICE EXPLOSION

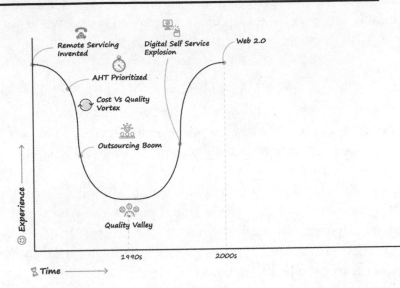

Following the Quality Valley of the 1990s, the rising acceptance of digital service and the practical and psychological benefits of self-service (convenience and agency) swung the CX arc back in an upward direction. Many companies started to believe they had found the perfect balance between decreasing the cost of service while increasing the quality of the experience.

But customers would soon come to expect even more and more digital functionality from the companies they chose to do business with, and this rise in expectations would bring with it an unintended consequence.

WHY THE "BOLT-ON" APPROACH DOESN'T CUT IT ANYMORE

As customers came to demand more digital options, and became increasingly comfortable with self-service functionality, it became harder for companies to keep up. The customer service "machine" at most organizations was designed originally for a nondigital world. Many of these newer digital options – most notably email and chat – were layered on top of a company's already-existing phone-based service platform, one at a time, as each became viable.

This non–integration of self-service on screens with live service on the phone has been described as a "bolt-on" approach – in which each channel operates like its own separate entity, often manned by separate teams.

With some agents doing phone service, some doing chat, others handling email, and so on – the result for many companies became a "multichannel" approach to service, based on a telephony-centric system that wasn't exactly *integrated*, so much as it was *infiltrated*.

Justin Robbins describes the evolution of digital service like a sci-fi movie in which the gravitational pull of the past is fighting against the zero-G weightlessness of the future, "In 1999, we had to do one thing well – phones. And then we started to use email. So at first we just had to add one more thing. And if we're being honest, even email wasn't *entirely* integrated. But then fast-forward to online ordering, through both the website and phone. Then social, SMS, webchat, video. We've seen the need to integrate so many more channels and systems and work streams so that a lot of the stuff that's making them run on the back end was slapped together in a way that wasn't clean or streamlined."

He adds, "At many companies, customer service started to look like a cardboard box covered in duct tape with a spring poking out one side, and a bungee cord wrapped around it. The cracks were being exposed. The spaceship started shuddering."

Tethr is an Austin-based company whose proprietary product is an AI-powered "conversation intelligence platform" that measures customer effort without the need for surveys or other customer feedback by processing voice analytics to assess whether a customer is experiencing a high- or low-effort interaction.

Matt Dixon (also a co-author of *The Effortless Experience*) now serves as Tethr's chief research and innovation officer. He says for many customers, the proliferation of digital channels has led to a new phenomenon: the "Digital Frustration Factor," which he defines as "how the customer feels about friction they encounter in online channels. It's another form of effort – the obstacles that get in the way of resolution. Tethr data shows customer effort scores are way worse when that person has had a bad *digital* experience – even worse than a bad *phone* experience."

As thousands of companies added more and more digital channels – no matter how hard they tried – the experience didn't always work as "seamlessly" as customers expected. In an attempt to make things better for customers, the overall experience in many cases became worse.

Roger Paulson adds, "A lot of people just expect technology and digital interactions to be magical and perfect. So when they're trying to figure out how to solve a problem and they can't find what they're looking for after 15 minutes, there's no magic. Digital channels aren't perfect – so far at least."

Compounding this challenge, the timeline for this proliferation of demand for self-service coincided with the first big upsurge in the popularity of social media. It soon became possible for *every* person's negative experience with *any* company to be shared in a way that would be visible to *everyone*.

- The number of easy opportunities for customers to complain about poor service experiences became much *higher*.
- The threshold for experiences that qualified as "complaint-worthy" became much *lower*.

SOCIAL MEDIA: SALT IN THE WOUND

Here's a reality we all know to be true – at some point in our society, it became acceptable for people to go online and "rip some company a new one." Watching a video of someone taking a wild swing at a big corporation, trying to knock the candy out of their multibillion-dollar piñata became a form of FUN!

Fun to do, fun to share with others, fun to witness.

Who remembers an early YouTube viral video titled "United Breaks Guitars?" That example has become so over-referenced that it is generally accepted as the first cell-division of the "We the People vs. The Companies of the World" part of our collective psyche.

Just in case you missed it:

- A musician is on a United Airlines flight from Chicago O'Hare en route to Omaha.
- As he is getting settled into his aisle seat, a window-seat passenger a few rows back is peering outside, saying, "Oh, man, one of those baggage guys just tried to throw a guitar into the cargo bin and missed!"
- The musician fumes during the entire flight knowing *his* $3,500 guitar was in "checked baggage" because it was too much of a hassle to try to squeeze it into the overhead bin.
- When he finally gets to baggage claim in Omaha – exactly as he already knew before he even opened the case – his pride and joy (a Taylor acoustic) is in pieces.
- He writes a song about it and posts the video online, just as YouTube is getting hot.
- He gets over 20 million views.
- Everyone feels sorry for the dude and laughs at how much United (and "the airlines") suck.
- Ranting on social media about bad service experiences becomes (and remains) click-bait catnip.

Nate Brown is the co-founder of CX Accelerator – he says every company has to accept the fact that many people now feel they have a social responsibility to "balance the scales" by somehow getting back at a company after a poor service experience. "It became a matter of justice. If we witness wrongdoing, we're gonna lash back out in whatever way we know how – Twitter, negative reviews, telling others. There's a blood debt. I am now actively looking to do damage to their organization. Do I have time to do this? No! But if this experience and that company has created such a debt – it must be paid. And I *will* find a way."

That sounds harsh, and rings with a slight tone of overdramatization because most companies report overall customer satisfaction (CSAT) over the past few years has been more than acceptably high. Virtually every company's VoC (voice of customer) data show that *most* customer interactions are good ones, or at least nominal.

So, how many people are *really* out there on social media ranting about bad experiences? It's got to be a low number, right? And it is. Another finding from the National Rage Study: 18 percent of consumers who complained about an issue took active steps to increase public awareness of their bad experience.[7] One out of five. That's not a bad ratio.

But it's the memorably bad stories that get socialized.

And when you think about what lies ahead in the next few years, consider the percentage of younger people who are becoming more socially active in reporting their negative customer experiences to others. It's certainly higher than 18 percent. A lot higher.

A 2019 report from Adobe showed that among US customers between 18 and 34 years old – 9 in 10 said they will take action after having a bad online customer experience, such as telling friends, stopping purchasing from the company, and posting negative reviews on social media. The data was based on a survey of 1,500 US adults regarding preferences and expectations for digital experiences in the retail, travel & hospitality, media and entertainment, and financial services industries.[8]

As if the socially ingrained negative psychological bias most people have about customer service wasn't enough of a pothole in the road, the "seamful" interactions customers were having with many of the new digital options fueled further negative experiences, which were exacerbated by viral transmission through social media.

Think of it as a kind of Moore's law – the negativity around customer service doubling every two years.

We Have Transformed into Digital-First Beings

The technology that enables us and the psychology that drives us are both pointed in the same direction – virtually all of us have become digital-first *people* now. Those who haven't transformed already are getting a little closer every year, or, are just getting on in years.

Therefore, the dynamics of meeting customers where they are and running a customer service operation are very different today. *But different doesn't always mean harder.* Once you understand the impact of the "peaks and valleys" in this ongoing evolution, then customer service as a function can finally (once and for all) get digital transformation right.

The service executives and leaders who have been the most successful so far and will continue to succeed over the next few years are those who see beyond just operational and economic considerations. They are the ones who are focusing on understanding the underlying psychological principles that drive customer behavior and loyalty – and how that psychology has been changing.

Customers still have a negative bias when they are engaging in a service interaction, but for *different reasons* now. Instead of their prevailing expectations being based on poor phone experiences they've had in the past, customers are now primarily frustrated by the "disconnection" between their online experience and what happens when they speak to a company representative. *This* is now the source of that inherent negativity.

And here's the thing – *that* is much easier to fix.

Committing to going all-in on rethinking the way you are providing digital customer service is not only more progressive, it's smart business. A study at MIT found that companies that have embraced digital transformation are 26 percent more profitable than their peers.[9]

And now the technology required to conduct all service interactions (even those that require a voice interaction) entirely on the customer's screen not only exists, but *is already starting to be used successfully* – not just by major national or global companies, but even by some smaller regional and local organizations.

As a result, they are dramatically changing the experience of serving their customers – from what was once "a customer service operation that had some digital elements," to a more evolved form – the name of which became the natural title for this book: **Digital Customer Service (DCS).**

Their firsthand experiences will be shared in the chapters to follow.

EVOLUTION OF CUSTOMER SERVICE: THE "EXPECTATION VALLEY"

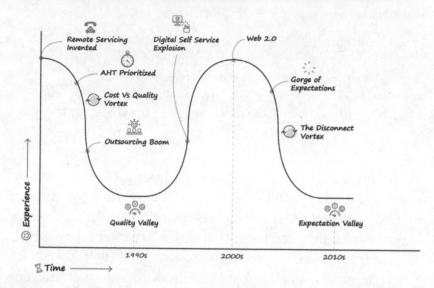

The advent of Web 2.0 represented a high-point for the customer experience as on-screen self-service became an alternative to having to call a company's call center. But expectations rose even more rapidly than most companies could keep up with, thus beginning a *channel race*. Since each new channel was "bolted-on" to the existing service platform – and none were integrated with phone service – customers and agents weren't "on the same page."

This mismatch between customer expectations and the reality of "seamful" digital experiences created the *disconnect vortex*.

Exacerbated by the visibility of poor experiences through social media, the overall reputation of customer service plummeted once more – but this time for *different reasons*.

In the Expectation Valley, most customers still harbored a negative bias about customer service, but the *source* of that negativity has evolved. Instead of being frustrated by long hold times, outsourced call centers and agents who tried to rush them off the phone, customers have become increasingly intolerant of the incongruity of multichannel experiences in which none of the various elements of the interaction seemed to be tied together.

KEY TAKEAWAYS: CHAPTER 3

■ *Digital self-service is now the dominant way people interact with companies.* After a slow start, customer acceptance of "serving myself" built momentum over time. Starting with the early introduction of the ATM, self-service exploded with the introduction of Web 2.0. Digital self-service allowed businesses to continue their journey of optimizing for costs but also created a significant increase in customer experience as it quickly resonated with people based on the convenience and agency self-service experiences provide.

■ *Customers want service experiences to take place on THEIR screen.* With the increased demand for digital self-service came higher customer expectations from their on-screen experiences. Businesses scrambled to introduce ways to digitally enhance these experiences, but this was generally done in an incremental (rather than transformative) fashion. The "bolt-on" approach is insufficient to meet the demands of customers who have already transformed.

■ *Poor service experiences are the ones that feel "seamful" to customers.* The nonintegration of digital self-service *on my screen* with live service *on the phone* created a mismatch between customer expectations and business realities. The solution: Businesses must meet customers where they are – on *their* screens. To achieve the goal of customer-centricity and achieve true loyalty, service must transform to become digital-centric rather than phone-centric.

Two

DCS Terminology Overview

This section is the "meat" of the book and consists only of **Chapter 4,** the most detailed of the seven.

Here we will explore each of the elements of a digital-first service model – with precise definitions, clear descriptions about what is so different, and practical examples of how DCS impacts real-life customer interactions.

In addition, we'll provide you with tools that will make it much more effortless for you to discuss digital transformation with your peers in IT, as well as with your CFO.

This is a section that digs into the fine details. If that's what you're looking for, you've come to the right place. If you're more of a skim-and-diver, take a quick flyover and dip into the areas that are most relevant to your interests and responsibilities.

At some level, what we'll be describing in this section might feel like some "aspirational vision of the future," but keep in mind that everything you'll be reading about is already a reality for those companies that are moving forward with the digital transformation of their customer service operations.

CHAPTER 4

The Three OnScreen Pillars of DCS

What we'll share in this chapter:

- While the term *digital customer service* has many meanings and interpretations, *Digital Customer Service (DCS)* refers to a specific software-driven solution that changes the nature of the customer interactions from phone-centric to digital-centric.

- DCS includes three categories of OnScreen Enhancements, which are the pillars of the overall experience:

  - OnScreen Communication
  - OnScreen Collaboration
  - OnScreen Automation

- Compared to other service models, DCS is not only more efficient and economical for companies, but virtually effortless for customers – which promotes long-term loyalty.

*"No sir, can you see that thing on your screen...you know...
it's like that gear-thingy...it's right HERE!*

...Wait, sir, are you even on OUR website?"

CLIMBING OUT OF THE VALLEY OF EXPECTATIONS

Are customer expectations out of control? Do people have a right
to expect companies to completely transform their entire service
models? *Is that really fair?*

But before you answer that question – don't. *The question
itself isn't fair.*

Customers want what they want, and they expect what they
expect. Whether *that's* fair isn't relevant. The reality is that customer
"taste" for digital service has evolved to the point where more and
more people now expect that *every* issue can and should be solved
on their screens – with *them* in total control of the interaction.

And when customers happen to run into a situation where that *isn't* true – because self-service isn't available for their specific issue, or they aren't confident they know how to complete a process within self-service – there's a serious *disconnect*.

So . . . now what?

In this chapter, we will explore what we've been learning about how companies can meet and even exceed this predominant customer expectation for more effortless digital experiences – and be accomplished in ways that also benefit the economics of the company.

EVOLUTION OF CUSTOMER SERVICE: THE INFLECTION POINT

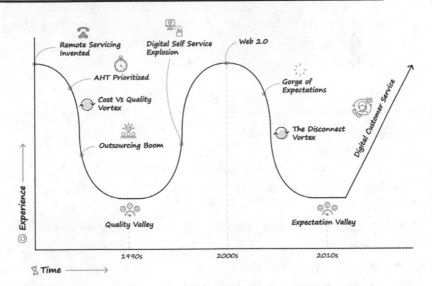

Brought on by the "cost vs. quality vortex," the service industry faced a **Quality Valley** in the 1990s – and the solution came from an unexpected source. While digital self-service was initiated as a cost-cutting strategy, as customers began transforming to a digital-first lifestyle, it quickly gained popularity and became the new standard for how service transactions should be engineered (increasing the experience to new heights).

But in the decade that followed, the experience of many customers cascaded downward to another low-point – the **Expectations Valley** – symbolized by the way customers "feel" when self-service was not an option despite expectations that everything should be self-servable.

(continued)

This was further compounded by the **Disconnect Vortex** – which meant many customers had the experience of interacting by phone with agents who had no visibility into everything they had already done online up until that point, forcing the customer to start their whole journey all over again. And up until recently, there was no practical way to escape the Expectation Valley.

Enter: Digital Customer Service.

The Generic Term "Digital Customer Service" Is a Monster Noun

Have you ever heard the term *monster noun*? In the business world, **monster nouns** are words (or terms) that virtually every company uses, but their exact definition and interpretation of value varies widely from one company to another, from leader to another within a company, or even one person to another on the same team.

These terms aren't monsters because they signify something *evil* or *out-to-getcha* – they most always refer to goals or outcomes that virtually every company *wants* to achieve.

EXAMPLE

One of the biggest monster nouns is "culture." The percentage of companies whose executives say they recognize the value of a strong culture rises every year. But the exact definition of what culture *is*, and exactly which strategies companies should be choosing to make progress against cultural goals are likely to be "all over the map."

That doesn't make culture unimportant – *it's critical* – but because of its varying interpretations, it can be hard for companies to reach agreement on exactly what they're trying to accomplish with their culture, and why it's so important. That's a problem.

Here are some other monster nouns that are important but hard to define exactly:

- Innovation
- Synergy
- Thought leadership

The problem with the monster noun ***digital customer service*** is that *anything* that uses the internet to enable *any* service functionality could be described as *digital customer service*.

But simply adding new digital functions to the existing service framework isn't sufficient to transform the customer experience to an on-screen world.

The reason for pointing out the variable interpretation of "digital customer service" is to contrast it with a much more specific noun – **DCS: Digital Customer Service.**

DCS DEFINED

DCS is a software platform that enables **OnScreen Enhancements** within any service interaction – regardless of where it starts – on a website, a mobile app, or via a dialed phone call.

In a self-service world, the screen is the center of the universe because that is where customers are. *The screen changes everything*.

Because most customers are now living a digital-first lifestyle, DCS is both the antidote to overcoming the negativity caused by the Expectations Valley, *and* the pathway to true digital transformation in customer service.

There are three types of OnScreen Enhancements in DCS:

1. OnScreen Communication
2. OnScreen Collaboration
3. OnScreen Automation

These are the three pillars that form the foundation of the DCS operating model.

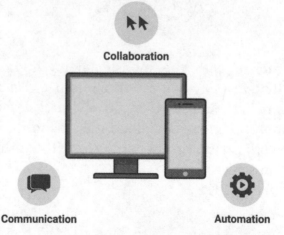

In DCS, the **customer's own screen** is "the stage" for the vast majority of interactions – even if an agent joins the discussion, they enter on the screen as well. Compared to service interactions that take place primarily on the phone, the visual nature of a DCS experience creates a number of advantages:

- *Efficiency*. Using OnScreen Enhancements, issues can be resolved at least 20 percent more quickly than an off-screen phone call, with some issues resolved up to 90 percent faster.

  - Using the customers' screen, agents can authenticate the customer's account faster, identify their issue more specifically and in many cases teach the customer how to serve themselves and/or avoid that same issue in the future.

  - When **phone agents** are transformed into **DCS agents** and work with customers on *their* screens, contact centers can often handle two to three times the number of interactions per agent – but in a way that is more engaging and even fun for agents themselves.

- *Effectiveness*. The visual nature of DCS makes sales conversion and upselling far easier. While most businesses already heavily rely on self-service in e-commerce, using OnScreen Enhancements increases conversion rates significantly.

  - Self-service purchase processes typically yield conversion rates in the 1–2 percent range – but when using DCS, conversion can increase to 8–10 percent or more.

- *Experience*. In our everyday lives we interact with friends, family, and colleagues using our screens every single day. *Why should a business interaction be any different?*

  - Dialing a phone number is becoming "a thing of the past" when we have the ability to communicate by voice or video right through our browsers.

- The experience of "meeting customers where they are" in this way has a marked impact on the metrics most closely linked to long-term loyalty.

- DCS organizations typically see an increase of over 15 points in Net Promoter Score (NPS) and achieve average Customer Satisfaction (CSAT) of 90+ percent.

Below are detailed descriptions of the three different types of OnScreen Enhancements within the DCS platform (communication, collaboration, automation).

OnScreen Communication

There are many ways that we use our screens to launch conversations – we text, we FaceTime, we message through social media, we Zoom (sometimes with video *on* and sometimes with video *off* – *while wearing our PJs!*).

These are all forms of **OnScreen Communication** – and all of these are available to customers in a DCS interaction.

OnScreen Communication

Core Components

	Chat and messaging	Real-time or asynchronous text-based messages that are exchanged through the company's primary website, portals, and mobile app. This includes live chat, in-app messaging, secure messaging, etc.

(continued)

Messaging via social media

Real-time or asynchronous text-based messages that are exchanged through the company's presence on third-party social media tools such as Facebook, Twitter, Instagram, Whatsapp, etc.

Messaging via SMS

Asynchronous text-based messages exchanged through a mobile device's native texting platform (including platforms such as Apple Business Chat).

Messaging via email

Asynchronous text-based messages exchanged through an email client. For certain industries, this also includes the use of a secure inbox within websites, portals, or mobile apps.

OnScreen Voice (digital)

Real-time verbal conversations launched from within the company's primary website, portals, or mobile app (imagine a video chat but with just the audio feed).

(continued)

OnScreen Voice
(callback)

Real-time verbal conversations launched from within the company's primary website, portals, or mobile app in which the customer inputs their number and receives a callback.

 Video chat

Real-time video conversation through the company's primary website, portals, or mobile app.

Interim Component / Bridging Functionality

 Near-screen
phone

One method for migrating dialed phone calls into DCS interactions is to guide those customers to a browsing session on a *nearby* computer or screen in order to introduce other OnScreen Enhancements.
This, of course, is a "bridge" step, but still works effectively to create a DCS experience. Over time, as fewer customers dial directly, this interim method will fade away.

A Note About "Voice" Interactions:

In the customer service world, the terms *phone* and *voice* are often used interchangeably. With the advent of DCS, this should no longer be the case. They are two different things:

- *Off-screen Phone.* A verbal interaction launched by dialing the digits of a phone number. This is also sometimes referred to as **inbound phone interactions**.
- *OnScreen Voice.* A verbal interaction that launches through a website, portal or app (either using digital voice or a phone callback).

The main advantage of **OnScreen Voice** is that it seamlessly becomes a part of the customer's already in-process digital session. The context of what the customer has been doing carries right through to the agent – and this makes the whole interaction feel effortless:

- An *off-screen phone call* requires the agent to gather information about the customer, authenticate them verbally, and request further information to understand their problem before getting to work on resolution.
- However, *OnScreen Voice* skips all of those preliminary steps because the customer has already been authenticated through the site, portal, or app, and the agent has full context of what the customer is trying to accomplish – so the agent can launch right into a personalized interaction that "meets the customer where they are."

OnScreen Voice vs. Off-Screen Phone Call

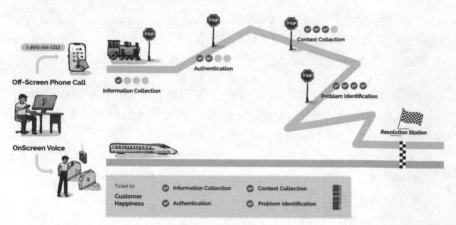

OnScreen Voice is the difference between taking the "local train" versus the "express train" to Resolution Station. Off-screen phone calls require the agent to collect information, authenticate the customer's account, and only then start to resolve the issue. But with OnScreen Voice, those steps have already occurred online, vastly expediting resolution and making the agent's job immeasurably more effortless.

OnScreen Collaboration

Websites and mobile apps are designed for customers to explore a company's digital domain on their own without guidance.

However, in situations where a customer is unsure how to navigate on their own, or has a question that's not in the company's FAQs, the customer has typically been relegated to having to dial a phone number to get additional assistance. This creates two distinctly different customer experiences – the *screen* experience and the off-screen *phone* experience – which are not linked in any way. That's a serious disconnect.

Imagine going to a museum, and as you're walking around you become interested in a particular exhibit and have a question – but there's no one there to help. So you walk

all the way back to the main entrance where there's a line
of five people ahead of you at the Information Desk, and
you finally get to talk to someone who asks, "How may I
help you?"

You say, "Can you send someone over to where I just
was – I have a question about this one exhibit," and she
says, "Yeah, we don't have anyone over there . . . but I have a
book here with descriptions of some of the newer exhibits –
can you describe exactly which one it was?"

And the whole time you're thinking, ". . . if there was
just someone over there WITH me, this would have been so
much easier . . ."

When customers are having trouble trying to resolve an issue
on a company's website or mobile app and are then forced to dial
a phone number – only to start all over again with an agent who
has no idea what they've been doing and isn't able to see what
they're seeing – it creates the same suboptimal dynamic. Everything the customer did on-screen before having to then make
a phone call to the company is perceived by the customer as a
waste of time.

But **OnScreen Collaboration** gives an agent full transparency into what's happening on the customer's screen – in
real time.

In the museum analogy it would be like if you were wearing
a GoPro as you walked around the gallery, and a helpful
docent (even if they were sitting in a remote location) could
see the exact exhibit you were looking at – in real time – and
*could answer all your questions. **That** is the essence of col-*
laboration in a digital environment.

There are several OnScreen Collaboration options:

OnScreen Collaboration

	Live Observation	The ability to view the customer's real-time browsing behavior on the company's primary website, portals, and mobile app (i.e., current page, scrolling, clicking, keystrokes, etc.).
	CoBrowsing	The ability to collaborate with the customer in real time using dual cursors on the website, portal, or app.
	Screen sharing	The ability to share pages or windows that are outside of the company's digital domain (i.e., external websites, social media, etc.).
	File sharing	The ability to securely scan and share files either in real time or asynchronously, using messaging or a secure inbox.

Note: With each of the OnScreen Collaboration options, customers must give their consent to participate. At no time does anyone from the company have access or visibility into anything the customer does not want to share. This should be clearly communicated to customers, because once it is, even those who may have been hesitant to engage in OnScreen Collaboration generally report this kind of interaction not only feels secure but creates a far superior experience.

OnScreen Automation

As customers navigate websites and apps – even though they are operating independently – there are a myriad of opportunities for companies to make that interaction more efficient and/ or to enhance the experience. **OnScreen Automation** triggers actions and responses on the customer's screen, based on data about *them* (from their past interactions or their browsing behavior in that moment).

For example: A "high value" customer is logged into their online banking portal and is exploring various mortgage options. Then they automatically receive an invitation to speak with a loan specialist – without even having to ask. This comes from DCS "predicting" the customer's likely next need and offering it proactively.

The possibilities are endless for tailoring interactions based on the phrasing a customer uses to describe their issue or their "digital body language" (more on that later).

The most important OnScreen Automation options are:

OnScreen Automation

	Visual authentication	Automated verification of the customer identity to an agent or bot using customer's log-in, or a single sign-on pop-up box.
	Chatbots	Automated single messages or conversations based on a customers' inquiries.

(continued)

	Pop-up messages	Automated informational dialogue boxes presented to a customer based on browsing behavior and/or business data captured in backend systems such as CRM (i.e., prior purchases, past browsing sessions).
	Invitations to interact	Automated invitations for a customer to connect with an agent based on browsing behavior and/or customer data. The customer still remains in total control.

OnScreen Enhancement "Combinations"

The ultimate utility of a DCS experience is best appreciated when considering how multiple OnScreen Enhancements can be woven together during a single interaction in a seamless combination. For instance:

- A customer initiates OnScreen Voice to verbally communicate with an agent through the online banking portal on the company's website
- The agent has no need to authenticate the customer (again!) because **visual authentication** has already automated the process
- The interaction is paired with **Live Observation** so the agent can instantly see the customer scrolling through the portal in real-time

The breadth of these various OnScreen Enhancement combinations creates unlimited possibilities, but it is the seamlessness of transitioning between them that makes a DCS so effective in creating a superior customer experience.

ONSCREEN COLLABORATION: GETTING ON THE SAME PAGE

A basic reality of customer service is that at the core of almost all interactions is some situation where "a person needs to *get* something or have something *fixed*." That, of course, can take a million different forms – everything from placing a simple order, to solving complex problems.

Because the screen is the focal point of DCS, OnScreen Collaboration creates an ease of communication that changes the nature of the interaction.

When two people are communicating back and forth to solve a problem, it is *way* easier for them to work together if they are looking at the same thing at the same time. It's so obvious, right?

Of course, that's not possible during a phone call. The interaction is reduced to a verbal articulation of one person trying to describe how to navigate a company's website, app, or portal taking them through various clicks and menus, without being certain the other person fully understands their instructions.

This, of course, often leads to confusion and an inefficient, frustrating interaction. And yet, virtually every company conducts thousands of interactions just like that every day.

Telling a customer how to perform a task they're unfamiliar with requires the agent to describe concepts and visuals that they are *very* familiar with, but the customer is not. It's tricky. *You know everything and they know nothing.*

To illustrate, let's compare the "degree of effectiveness" of a common task that requires *one person* who is very familiar with something, to describe it to *another person* who has no knowledge:

EXAMPLE

You invite a friend to your home who has never been there before. A few minutes after they were scheduled to arrive, they call to say they think they're lost and need your help. (And – for the sake of this example – let's imagine that they don't have access to GPS.)

The following are three different ways you could help guide your friend – and for each, let's imagine the same scenario as it would relate to a customer service interaction. We will assign a letter grade to each method based on the effectiveness of the communication.

Describing Directions from Memory

Driving Directions:
"OK, based on what you're telling me, it sounds like you're going the wrong way on Central Blvd. That's no good. See if you can turn around. You should go for about 5 minutes . . . and then you're gonna see a gas station on the right – I think it's an Exxon station, it used to be Sunoco, but I think they changed it last month.

Customer Service Interaction:
This would be like an agent who has navigated a company's website so many times it has become second-nature to them and is trying to describe things to a person who is unfamiliar with the site. This is sometimes called **the curse of knowledge**.

(continued)

That's Sunrise Highway. You're gonna want to make a right there, and then an immediate left on Walnut Ave. We're about halfway down the street on the left; it's 801 Walnut."

It is hard to relate to another person who knows nothing when you're trying to describe something you've seen a million times. And, BTW, what happens when the website is updated?

Grade = C–

Looking at Google Street View

Driving Directions:
"I think the problem is that you might be going west on Central Blvd. Do you see a Burger King coming up on the right? OK, then you're definitely going the wrong way. See if you can turn around. Good.

Now you should see a Ford car dealership on the right – are you seeing that? Now you're going east on Central, so you're good. Go for about another 5 minutes or so. Soon you'll be passing a Safeway grocery store on the right. When you see that, the next major road past the Safeway is Sunrise Highway . . . there's gonna be an Exxon station on the right. You'll be making a right there. Tell me when you're there . . ."

Customer Service Interaction:
This is the most common scenario in customer service. The agent is looking at the company's website on their own screen in the Contact Center, and the customer is looking at the site but on their screen. There are more visual descriptions being offered, but no certainty that the customer is looking at the same thing as the agent.

Definitely better – but again, the success of the interaction depends on both parties looking at the same version of the website or app and the same layout (mobile vs. desktop vs. tablet).

Grade = B–

Looking at a Live Feed from a Dash-Cam Inside Your Friend's Car

---

Driving Directions:
"Hey, I can see you're going the wrong way on Central Blvd. No problem. Get in the left lane . . . see that turnaround up ahead, yeah, behind that red pickup in the left lane . . . yeah, make a U-turn there. That's it . . . now you're headed in the right direction.
Your next turn is about a mile ahead, and you'll be making a right, so continue staying in the right lane, right behind that blue BMW who's in front of you. That's exactly where you want to be. You're just about 5 minutes out, and I will guide you the rest of the way . . ."

Customer Service Interaction:
This is the closest thing to being IN the car with the driver. Both people are seeing the same thing at the same time.
In customer service this is why OnScreen Collaboration creates such a superior experience – for both the customer AND the agent.
Being on the same screen changes everything.
Grade = A+

As you can see from the above examples, without Live Observation and CoBrowsing there is *no way* to guarantee that the customer and agent are looking at the same thing – even if they *think* they are. Plus, websites, portals, and apps change constantly. Updates get pushed through, the use of geo-targeting alters certain versions of the site for marketing purposes, and those are all positive developments in an organic digital environment. But when working with customers who aren't daily users, the way various pages lay out on different devices (laptop, tablet, smartphone) can appear very different or change over time. What could be more frustrating?

But what could be faster, more efficient, or more reassuring for customers than for an agent to instantly "pop on my screen"? who knows *who* you are, *what* you're doing, and is also enabled to look at *your* screen in real time. That is the literal definition of *being on the same page* but executed in a digital way.

Live Observation and CoBrowsing solve for the miscommunication that occurs when trying to help customers navigate a company's website or app, in ways that dramatically decrease effort – not just what customers have to do, but more importantly how it feels.

Q: Is "being on the same page" better for the *customer* who is enabled to navigate a website or app by themselves with the helpful guidance of a friendly agent? Or, is it better for the *agent* who doesn't have to guess whether the customer is seeing the same thing they are?

A: *Trick question. It's best for both.*

DCS in Action: CoBrowsing Creates Major Efficiency Improvements

Profile
- Software company (B2B)
- 500 employees

The benefits of CoBrowsing for this company are twofold:
- Making it easier for their agents to teach customers how to use their software
- Helping teach customers how to teach *their* clients to use the software

(continued)

This company offers an online software platform that is used mostly by financial analysts, and because it is based on a very sophisticated data set, it is constantly being updated. This has traditionally driven heavy customer service call volume as customers typically have trouble navigating certain features when changes are made to various functions and updates are pushed.

After implementing DCS, their service team immediately began offering customers the option to CoBrowse in these situations – and those OnScreen experiences were an immediate hit.

The ability to "teach" customers how to use the software more effectively by looking at the customer's screen together, and sharing information about how to solve issues entirely in self-service, created a dramatic change in the company's "interaction mix."

Before DCS, only about 20 percent of customer service issues were handled entirely in a digital-centric way. Within a little more than a month, the company reported the mix had already shifted to 50/50. In less than a year, the ratio was closer to 80/20.

Within the service team, enabling agents to put the service experience "on the customer's screen" transformed the customer service job into much more of a "teaching" role, and had an immediate impact on the efficiency of many interaction types. In the most dramatic example, an "issue type" that often took as many as 10 minutes to complete in a phone-only interaction was cut down to as low as 2 minutes when both the customer and agent were looking at navigation and functionality together.

Plus, since many of their customers need to teach *their own clients* how to use the software, the visual element of these

(continued)

DCS interactions are reportedly making many clients much more confident in their ability to be successful themselves.

The company reported significant gains in NPS for these digital interactions and both customers and agents are saying the changeover has created a more effortless experience in virtually every live interaction.

Company executives say they believe the transformation to DCS has become a true differentiator among their competitors, and they are continuing to expand their use of OnScreen Enhancements to cover an ever-wider range of customer interactions.

DIGITAL-ALSO VS. DIGITAL-ONLY VS. DIGITAL-FIRST

There are three different strategies for how DCS can be implemented. And while any of these strategies would be better than *not* adjusting to the expectations of increasingly digital customers – as you can see from the chart below, these three are ranked in order of increasing effectiveness – each is better than the previous one.

Strategy	Description
Digital-Also 📞 Phone-First Platform | 🖥️ DCS Modules	This strategy starts with a traditional phone-first or call center software system. For companies that have traditionally used the phone as the primary entry point to connect with customers, adding digital options provides on-screen benefits.

(continued)

Pros:

- Leveraging an existing software system already in place.
- Specialized teams become focused on handling different interaction types (phone, chat, SMS, email).

Cons:

- Siloed management of different interaction types. This typically results in routing rules or data dashboards that are incongruous and difficult to analyze.
- Creates a disjointed experience for customers and agents when moving from one type of interaction to another (i.e., transitioning from a chat interaction to a voice interaction).

Digital-Only

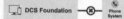

This strategy starts with a text-based digital interaction in live chat, social messaging, or a chatbot-centric system. For companies that have created a service strategy around minimizing or eliminating phone interactions, it can be beneficial to add further on-screen functionality.

Pros:

- Resolving interactions at the point of origin.
- Lower cost-to-serve.

Cons:

- Voice and video experiences are not well integrated or unavailable.
- Complex issues can create higher effort to resolve without the ability to "just talk to someone," which leads to frustration and potential disloyalty.

Digital-First

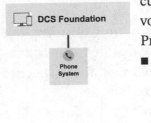

A system designed to primarily interact with customers digitally but *also* incorporating voice as a fully integrated option.

Pros:

■ It facilitates seamless transitions (i.e., start with chat, then add voice or video) while maintaining full context for both customers and agents throughout the interaction.

■ Routing, reporting, and administration are managed in a single system that treats digital and voice interactions in the same way.

Cons:

■ Digital-first requires replacement or consolidation of systems (to be conducted either incrementally or all at once).

■ Change management and retraining is required for traditional phone agents to become successful in conducting digital interactions.

Since one of the primary goals of DCS is to migrate away from phone-based service interactions, any time your agents are taking a phone call (in situations where the customer is on or near a screen) you're losing! Again, this does *not* mean avoiding voice conversations, it means transitioning from blind off-screen phone calls to OnScreen Voice interactions in which the customer and agent are on the same page.

DCS meets customers *where they are*: Wherever they first entered, where they are in the midst of their resolution journey at that moment, and where they are psychologically in their evolution to a digital-first lifestyle.

HOW TO BUILD A BUSINESS CASE FOR DCS

In Chapter 1, we shared a "back of the envelope" formula as a basic sketch of the cost-efficiency created by transforming to a DCS service model. In this section, we've expanded this framework in greater detail to enable you to get a much more specific look at the potential cost savings for your company.

What will you need? Assessing the potential business value of transforming to DCS requires you to gather (or at least to start by estimating) three sets of data:

1. *Call data/cost.* Calculate the total number of minutes all agents are interacting with all customers by phone. Calculate your total staff budget (including all-in expenses for benefits, paid leave, other HR costs).
2. *DCS opportunities.* Determine the percentage of:
   - Phone callers who are already on/near a screen
   - Those customers who *could* have resolved their issue in self-service if they knew how and were confident they could
3. *DCS OnScreen benefits.* Calculate the cost savings and efficiency boost of using OnScreen Communication, Collaboration, and Automation.

Below is a more detailed example of how this tool can be used to calculate potential ROI. We hope you are already thinking about doing this same exact exercise with your team, to see what kind of cost-efficiency may be available to your DCS operation.

EXAMPLE

The company is a regional bank. While the service team transitioned over time to become a "multichannel" operation (with some agents handling basic chat sessions and email interactions) the vast majority are still focused on answering off-screen phone calls. They operate a call center with 80 FTEs and an annual staff budget of $4.8 million.

Call Data	
Off-screen phone calls (annual)	862,056
AHT (mins)	5.75
Total annual off-screen phone volume (mins)	4,952,512

Over the past few years, the bank has created a self-service portal where customers can log in to see their account details, as well as access additional functionality like ordering checks, reviewing transactions, finding the bank's routing number, changing beneficiaries, conducting transfers between accounts, and submitting loan applications among others.

So, what percentage of off-screen phone customers were already on or near a screen as they're having trouble completing a transaction?

Think about it this way: Where do most customers even *get* your customer service phone number in the first place? Likely from either your website or mobile app, or through a search engine like Google. What this means is that they are already *on a screen,* but they are still being treated like a "phone customer."

Of course, most companies don't have a specific metric to determine the percentage of phone callers that are on or near a screen, but it is likely high. Industry averages indicate it is typically in the 70–80 percent range. One suggestion: Start by asking your agents. They will likely have a sense based on their experience. Any customer whose issue involves your website or app is likely looking at a screen as they're calling. This represents a missed opportunity. In terms of your own calculations, it is more than OK to use an approximation based on anecdotal information or to start with the benchmark above.

DCS Opportunities

% Off-screen phone calls where customer is on/near a screen	80%
% on/near-screen calls with issues resolvable in self-service	70%
Off-screen phone time addressable with OnScreen Collaboration (min)	2,773,407

If 80 percent of off-screen phone customers are on or near a screen, and 70 percent of those people could have potentially solved their issue in self-service (if they only knew how, or were confident enough to do it themselves) that means *56 percent of the total number of "live phone minutes"* the bank is spending every year, is like sand slipping through their fingers.

This means nearly 2.8 million minutes of talk time could benefit from OnScreen Collaboration.

Instead of an agent having to guess where the customer is struggling, OnScreen Collaboration would shave at least a few minutes off the total talk time of that interaction by giving the agent a real time view into this customers' session on the website, portal or mobile app. A conservative estimate would be that this could reduce the time of these interactions by approximately 30 percent.

DCS Benefits (OnScreen Collaboration)

% Time savings using OnScreen Collaboration	30%
Off-screen phone time saved with OnScreen Collaboration (min)	832,022
Annual savings	$520,014
FTE increased capacity	117%

The actual time savings created by OnScreen Collaboration is, of course, dependent on the complexity of the self-serve experience. For instance, walking a customer through a series of transfers from multiple accounts over the phone could take 8–10 minutes. With OnScreen Collaboration, however, that duration could easily be cut in half as the agent shows the customer exactly how to make the change.

As an overall average, DCS companies report that OnScreen Collaboration reduces off-screen phone call time by around 30 percent (and – as customers become more digitally self-sufficient, the numbers only get better).

And so far, this only calculates the cost savings from transforming live agent interactions into OnScreen Collaboration opportunities – but in this case that is already $520,000/year.

Another calculation to determine the full value of OnScreen Enhancements is to evaluate the impact of OnScreen Automation. In this example, approximately 20 percent of live phone interactions *could* have been automated – to create a customer experience that would be even faster and require less effort.

DCS Benefits (OnScreen Automation)

% Low complexity off-screen phone calls deflected by chatbot	20%
Off-screen phone time saved with OnScreen Automation (min)	990,502
Annual savings	$619,064
FTE increased capacity	120%

So between OnScreen Collaboration and OnScreen Automation, transforming to DCS represents a conservative annual cost savings of $520,000 (collaboration) + $619,000 (automation) or nearly $1.4 million/year on a staff budget of $4.8 million.

NOTE: Two other considerations that are not even included in this business case but are worth considering:

- The efficiencies of OnScreen Communication in reducing handle time (concurrent messaging interactions or OnScreen Voice for example)
- The overall reduction in future live contact volume driven by customers becoming more digitally self-sufficient

In later chapters, we will introduce you to service leaders from a number of DCS companies who are reporting considerable success in creating greater efficiency in the moment, while also decreasing the need for live assistance in the future.

What Would You Do with That Kind of Cost Efficiency?

In the above example, within just the first year of transforming to a DCS model, this regional bank would save about 30 percent of its staff operating budget. That represents a massive opportunity, and also puts into play a number of choices for service executives to consider.

While any of the following might be a good move, which do you think would be best for *your* company?:

- *Give back the savings.* Reduce your operating budget and headcount (ideally by attrition, rather than downsizing) and operate a leaner, meaner staffing model while contributing the savings back to the company's overall bottom line.
- *Invest the savings back into making your team stronger.* Maintain headcount but pay frontline agents a higher salary. If that was possible, could you reduce turnover and retain your

best people longer? Could you attract better, more qualified candidates? What about enabling more and better training in areas like upselling and cross-selling? Could you create a true "digital-first service team" instead of a "service team that does a few digital things?"

- *Split the difference.* Some combination of reduced overall operating costs plus building an upgraded service team might be the best of both worlds.

If achieving this kind of fiscal efficiency came at the cost of a slightly *worse* customer experience, well . . . it might still be justifiable. *But the exact opposite is true.* Companies that have gone all-in on DCS say they are not only running a much more cost-efficient service operation, they are also creating a far superior experience for their customers.

Added Bonus: DCS Is More Secure

The **security** of personal customer information is a critical priority for every company. Just think back to recent news stories of companies that have suffered data breaches or had rogue employees stealing customer identities to imagine the kinds of nightmares these incidents create for service executives – not to mention their counterparts in Legal.

In a DCS environment, the possibility of data theft is minimized to the lowest level of risk.

An agent should never have to request a customer's personal data directly, because by the time an agent enters an interaction with a customer, they have likely already been authenticated through the company's website or mobile app.

But even if that isn't the case, by using OnScreen Enhancements, the agent can direct the caller to a digital property to enter their information. Any text a customer enters is displayed to the agent in real-time; however, **sensitive personal data** is automatically masked.

An OnScreen approach to data security also prevents potential issues linked to call recording or ambient overhearing. For example, when customers are required to share credit card information, if the customer is announcing their account number verbally, there are a host of risks:

- The agent could write the information on a scratch pad and use it later.
- The agent's computer where they manually type in the information could be corrupted.
- A screen recording platform could be used to steal information.
- A CCTV system could be capturing audio or video of a customer's personal information.
- The physical environment around the agent poses the possibility that someone else is listening in (especially in a work-from-home service operation).
- Anyone within the customer's earshot could be listening surreptitiously.

While the cost-efficiency of DCS is the primary motivation for most companies to transform their service operations, enhanced security is an additional benefit that should be considered as well.

Get Your Agents to Stop Asking This One Question

It's a simple question. Innocuous, really. Asked in all sincerity, and with all the best intentions. But for an increasing percentage of customers, it's a question that can set a service interaction off on a negative high-effort note from the get-go:

"How may I help you?"

How could that *possibly* be harmful? It's the question that initiates virtually every live customer interaction, and it has for years.

But that's the problem.

These changes in digital habits and customer behavior require companies to confront a new reality of interacting with customers. With the proliferation of self-service functionality, most customers are well into what they perceive as the *middle* of their resolution journey before they ever speak to or chat with a live agent.

Now can you see how this question – asked innocently and even with the kindest tone of voice and the greatest of soft-skills – could be the *worst* thing to ask a customer?

Think about it this way: When you're in the middle of some activity (telling a story, watching a movie, playing a game) and someone else barges in and expects you to start all over so *they* can catch up, how does that make you *feel*?

But this is the situation customer service agents find themselves in every day – barging into the middle of a customer's digital journey without any context about that person or their issue.

That is a high-effort experience. But it doesn't have to be. Not anymore.

With the advent of DCS and OnScreen Enhancements, if an agent joins a customer in the midst of an interaction, everything the customer has already been doing across the company's entire digital landscape can be made visible to the agent.

When the agent already knows *who* they are engaging with, and *what* that customer is trying to accomplish, the conversation becomes faster, more efficient, and more effortless as a result.

So, you need to deliver a eulogy for "How may I help you?"

It had a good run. It served us well for decades. But we – and our customers – live in a very different world today.

If you want customers to be loyal, you need to serve them in the fastest, most effortless way possible. You need to meet them where *they* are – instead of where *you* are.

KEY TAKEAWAYS: CHAPTER 4

■ *The same three words express very different concepts.* While the term "digital customer service" can be translated as "anything that makes service more digital," Digital Customer Service is a software platform that seamlessly integrates OnScreen Enhancements. This changes the focal point of a service interaction to *the customer's own screen* – the same place where it started.

■ *OnScreen Communication, Collaboration, and Automation are the three "pillars" of DCS.* These OnScreen Enhancements can be enabled through any entry point – and while each fulfills a different function, they are all designed to increase the efficiency and effectiveness of a service interaction (typically reducing staff operating costs by about one-third), while *also* creating a markedly better customer experience.

■ *"Phone" and "Voice" are not the same thing.* While an increasing percentage of service interactions can be automated or conducted entirely in self-service, live communication between a customer and an agent is often the best way to resolve more complex issues. But that doesn't mean it has to take place on the phone. OnScreen Voice (or in some cases video chat) enables the same 1-to-1 personal experience, but without the need to discontinue a digital interaction and start all over again on the phone.

■ *You must adopt a digital-first mindset.* The vast majority of customers have evolved to a lifestyle in which their smartphone, laptop, tablet (or often some combination) are tethered to them at all times. Companies need to evolve just as quickly by adopting a DCS strategy that is also digital-first – not just digital-also, or even digital-only.

Three

DCS Transformation Overview

The DCS service model has been designed as both the "antidote" to the enduring negative mindset most people have when they are contacting Customer Service as well as the pathway for digital-first customer interactions.

But transforming to DCS service operation isn't just a matter of installing new software or completing a switchover to a new system. To succeed, companies need to adapt to a different *mindset*.

Over the final three chapters, we will share practical information and "things you can do" to create maximum success in the months and years ahead, by exploring the three most important considerations of *any* transformation:

■ **Chapter 5: The Process**
  ■ What is the process for transforming the service operation from a platform that was created originally for phone-first interaction (or even "face-to-face"), to one that optimizes to digital-first customer interactions?

■ **Chapter 6: The People**
  ■ How does transforming to a DCS service model impact the people who interact directly with customers (including your "virtual agents") – as well as those who lead and manage them?

■ **Chapter 7: The Positioning**
  ■ How does the transformation to a DCS service strategy position companies differently, in ways that create greater competitive advantage?

Throughout these chapters, we will introduce you to a host of tools, exercises, and diagnostics that will enable you to take the practical steps to accelerate the digital transformation of your service operation.

CHAPTER 5

The Process –
A Step-by-Step Guide

What we'll share in this chapter:

■ How can your company migrate from a communications platform that was designed to power phone-first customer service, to a platform that powers a digital-first experience?

■ What are the essential elements you will need in order to engineer seamless shifts back-and-forth between virtual assistance and live assistance – across all communication modes?

■ How should you design the Digital Customer Service "journeys" you want to create for your customers to maximize their future loyalty?

■ What metrics will help you know if you're moving in the right direction – for the mutual benefit of your company, your customers and your employees?

PUT IT ON THE SCREEN

The key to getting as far away from off-screen phone calls as you can get, is to discover how to fulfill almost all service interactions in the **on-screen environment** – including issues that are best served through a verbal discussion with an agent. Again, this hasn't been possible or practical until recently.

Here's a way to think about the future of service: If a customer is *on or near a screen* – they should never need to engage in an off-screen phone interaction ever again.

The transformation from a phone-first model to a digital-first model requires service and digital leaders to rethink the process of how customers complete tasks and resolve issues in online interactions – and (of course) not just to think *about* customers, but to think *like* them.

- What are they coming to your website, portals, or mobile app to *do*?
- Which *processes* can they complete in self-service, and which require agent assistance?
- What is their *mindset* as they are beginning each given process?

The goal in DCS is to turn each service interaction into a "curated journey" that creates the lowest-effort experience for customers, but in the most economically efficient way for the company.

> Ultimately you need to engineer digital journeys for your customers that not only achieve resolution but also create **loyalty-building experiences**.

And as aspirational as that may sound – it is now possible. Here's an analogy that may help you envision what lies ahead as you continue to evolve your digital strategy.

"COOKING UP" THE IDEAL DIGITAL SERVICE STRATEGY

Let's use a relatable comparison: Instead of being a service, CX, or digital leader responsible for transforming to a digital-first operating environment, what if you were an executive chef charged with developing a concept for a new restaurant?

In order to create your culinary strategy, you would need to follow three primary steps:

- Step 1: Make sure you have access to a variety of excellent ingredients.
- Step 2: Learn more about your customers' taste(s) so you can experiment with different dishes that use your ingredients in the most appealing and efficient way.

- Step 3: Once you know what people like best, consistently serve *those* dishes.

To translate this to the goal of transforming to a DCS service model:

- *Step 1: Get the right ingredients.* Acquire the capability to introduce OnScreen Enhancements to add visual clarity to any digital process.
- *Step 2: Learn which dishes people like best.* Test various digital journeys using customer reaction and feedback to continually improve your ability to refine your recipes.
- *Step 3: Serve your best dishes consistently.* As you continue to better understand which combinations of OnScreen Enhancements best suit your customers' needs and expectations, focus on consistently delivering excellent digital service experiences that will drive greater loyalty.

In this section we will offer a number of frameworks and exercises that will enable you to accomplish each of these steps.

1. Get the Right Ingredients   *2. Learn Which Dishes People Like*   *3. Serve Your Best Dishes Consistently*

STEP 1: GET THE RIGHT INGREDIENTS

Each OnScreen Communication, Collaboration, or Automation enhancement should be thought of as an individual *ingredient* – to be mixed in different ways to create a wide variety of personalized customer journeys.

DCS provides a menu of OnScreen ingredients that can be tailored to the unique taste of *each customer* based on the specific interaction or process they're engaging in at the moment.

Your company should be thinking about the various combinations of information, guidance, and interaction you could introduce at any/every phase of a customer's journey to make it more effortless. Although a customer is "on their own" in digital self-service, that doesn't mean they don't want to be guided to the fastest pathway to resolving their issue.

So, to refine the "recipes" for various customer journeys, you need to know what kinds of digital experiences will work best for which situations – and to assess whether your current vendors and partners are capable of providing you with each of the ingredients you need.

The Digital Customer Service Journeys Grid

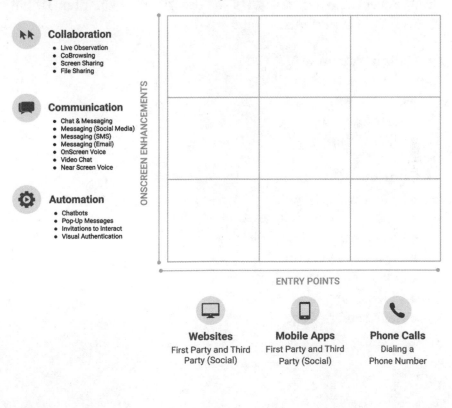

Starting along the bottom from left to right (the *x*-axis), these are the **entry points** – three different options a customer can choose as they initiate a contact:

- *Websites.* The customer goes directly to the company's website, logs into their account or they visit a third-party site (i.e., social media outlet)
- *Mobile apps.* The customer clicks on the company's app or logs into their account through a first or third-party app (i.e., social media outlet)
- *Phone calls.* The customer dials your service number via a mobile phone (where they are on a screen already) or a landline (in situations where they are likely near a computer). Also known as off-screen phone (as described in Chapter 3).

Then from top to bottom (the *y*-axis) are the three categories of **OnScreen Enhancements** (as described in Chapter 3) that create a DCS experience:

- **Collaboration**
  - Live Observation
  - CoBrowsing
  - Screen sharing
  - File sharing

- **Communication**
  - Chat and messaging
  - Messaging via social media
  - Messaging via SMS
  - Messaging via email
  - OnScreen Voice
  - Video chat
  - Near-Screen Voice

- **Automation**
  - Chatbots
  - Pop-up messages
  - Invitations to interact
  - Visual Authentication

There are dozens of different customer journeys a company could create – starting in *any* entry point, and adding *any number* of additional OnScreen Enhancements along the way. This grid should be thought of as the "map" to plot those digital journeys.

But first, you must determine whether your service platform includes all the basic ingredients you will need. And as you assess your current capabilities, the key question is not just "Which digital channels do we have?" but "Do we have the capability for a customer to seamlessly shift between them?"

As you conduct your assessment of DCS capabilities, the likeliest conclusion you will reach is: *"We have some of these capabilities, but not all of them. And if we're being honest the ones we have aren't tied together very well."*

If so, consider the options for acquiring the ingredients you will need, and think about how they connect to each other. Which of these already exist in some other form, or are being used by another function within your company? Which can we create in-house? Which will require assistance from vendors? Which vendor strategy makes the most sense: Finding individual suppliers who can provide one or a few of these capabilities, or a vendor who can provide a suite of tools to fill out your digital inventory list?

One resource that may be helpful – an RFP (request for proposal) inventory checklist specific to digital transformation in customer service. There's an interactive tool available on the website digitalcustomerservicerfp.com – it includes a checklist for both *customer-facing* and *back-office* digital functionality.

How to Use the Grid to Create Seamless DCS Journeys

Let's use the Digital Customer Service Journeys Grid to envision five typical customer scenarios. While each covers a different combination of entry points and OnScreen Enhancements – the one thing all five have in common is that within each journey the transitions all occur in a completely seamless way.

For each of these scenarios, take note of the opportunities that occur during the course of each interaction:

- To decrease customer effort, improve the quality of the customer experience, and increase customer loyalty
- To reduce the cost of *this* interaction, as well as *future* interactions with this customer

As we "go along on the journey" with each customer, we will start at that person's entry point (*to meet the customer where they are*) then follow them through various OnScreen Enhancement options introduced at specific moments.

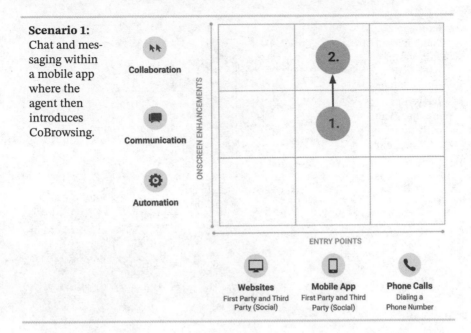

Scenario 1: Chat and messaging within a mobile app where the agent then introduces CoBrowsing.

Collaboration

Communication

Automation

ONSCREEN ENHANCEMENTS

2.

1.

ENTRY POINTS

Websites
First Party and Third
Party (Social)

Mobile App
First Party and Third
Party (Social)

Phone Calls
Dialing a
Phone Number

Jake, a policy holder at Gotyurback Insurance, logs into the carrier's mobile app to submit a claim after a fender bender but is not sure how to complete the process.

1. Jake chooses in-app messaging to start a chat conversation with a claims adjuster.
2. The adjuster offers to help Jake fill out the claim form on-screen by offering CoBrowsing, and they complete the process together (also teaching Jake how to do it himself next time, which is easy!).

[*Fast forward:* The claim is submitted much faster than he expected and Jake happily gives top scores in a post-interaction satisfaction survey.]

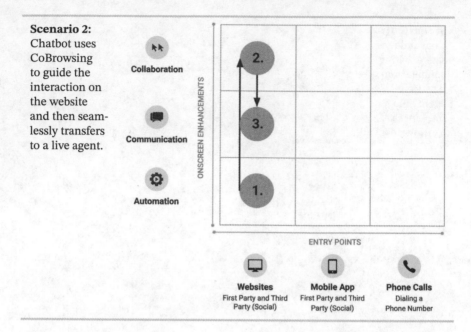

Scenario 2: Chatbot uses CoBrowsing to guide the interaction on the website and then seamlessly transfers to a live agent.

Shawna has heard great things about Memberific Credit Union, so she visits its public website to learn about applying to join:

1. After detecting that Shawna has been on the Member Benefits page for a while, a chatbot offers to interact, sensing that she lives in the right geography and is probably interested in membership.
2. During the interaction, the bot offers to navigate Shawna to the member application and guide her through the process on-screen.
3. When the bot realizes it can't answer one of Shawna's questions, it automatically connects her to a live agent who has full context of the chat and continues the journey without missing a beat. The agent communicates through OnScreen Voice to talk Shawna through the rest of the application process.

[*Fast forward:* Five years from now, she is still a member, and over time has recommended Memberific to her sister and two friends, who are now also members.]

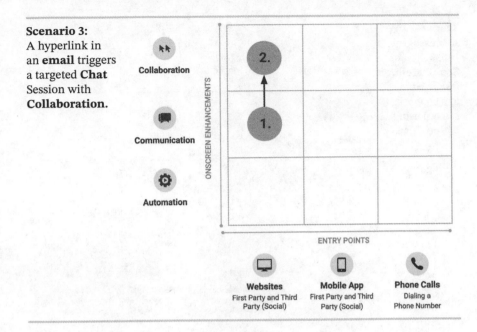

Scenario 3: A hyperlink in an **email** triggers a targeted **Chat** Session with **Collaboration.**

Collaboration

Communication

Automation

ONSCREEN ENHANCEMENTS

ENTRY POINTS

Websites
First Party and Third Party (Social)

Mobile App
First Party and Third Party (Social)

Phone Calls
Dialing a Phone Number

Late one evening, **Cecil** is exploring the Local University website hoping to learn about summer film production programs. Cecil finds an email address for admissions and decides to give it a shot – sending an email with many questions about the program, including how to apply:

1. A representative at the university reads Cecil's message and sends a reply with a link to a page that has more details on the program options. When Cecil visits the page, the link triggers a routing request to have an available admissions agent proactively offer a chat session to assist.
2. Once the two are messaging, the admissions counselor offers CoBrowsing to show Cecil all the different options that the film program has to offer and helps him fill out his application. The entire experience takes place on Cecil's screen.

[*Fast forward:* Shortly after graduating from the program, Cecil receives his award for Best Short Film at the Sundance Film Festival and thanks the fine folks at Local University in his acceptance speech.]

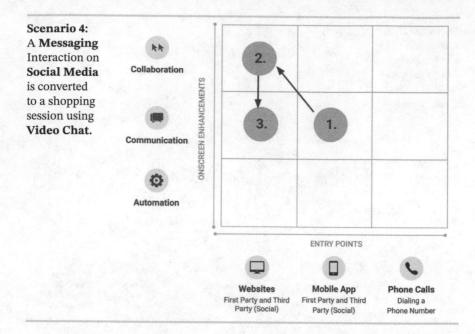

Scenario 4: A **Messaging** Interaction on **Social Media** is converted to a shopping session using **Video Chat.**

Barry got a promotion last month and wants to treat himself to a luxury watch. He is idly browsing through the Pinnacle Luxury Wear page on Facebook.

1. Barry decides to message Pinnacle through the Facebook app to help him decide which watch is right for him.
2. A helpful specialist sends Barry a link to the website and offers to show him some options in the catalog via a CoBrowsing Session.
3. When Barry narrows down his choices, he decides to request an OnScreen callback so he can go deeper into the details of this big purchase. The two talk for a bit when the specialist offers to upgrade to a video chat to reinforce the personalized white-glove service.

[*Fast forward:* Barry now buys all his dress shirts custom-made, with the left sleeve a half-inch shorter so his Rolex is always poking out. He recommends Pinnacle in an eight-shot photo essay on his Instagram account.]

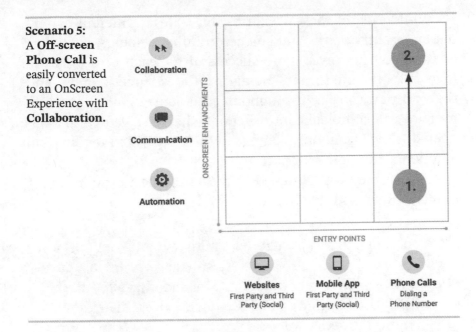

Scenario 5:
A **Off-screen Phone Call** is easily converted to an OnScreen Experience with **Collaboration.**

Collaboration

Communication

Automation

ONSCREEN ENHANCEMENTS

ENTRY POINTS

Websites
First Party and Third
Party (Social)

Mobile App
First Party and Third
Party (Social)

Phone Calls
Dialing a
Phone Number

Alicia is logged onto the Sunshine Travel website to make some changes to an upcoming group vacation to Aruba she booked a few weeks ago for herself and three friends. But as she is trying to make these changes, she realizes she needs assistance with some of the details.

1. Alicia dials the Sunshine Travel toll-free number and is connected to an agent, who is able to see her customer record based on her phone number and is then able to see the details of her current browsing session.
2. The agent asks if Alicia would like on-screen help completing the change. Alicia accepts, and together they easily modify the trip using CoBrowsing, to her great delight.

[*Fast forward:* At a pool party in Aruba, Alicia's group runs into a bachelor party group, where she meets Allan, a quirkily attractive executive from Denver – who, as it turns out, is the head of Service for Sunshine Travel! The wedding is next June.]

While each of these scenarios illustrates a different combination of entry points and OnScreen Enhancements, every one of these journeys was more successful for each of the parties involved – the **customer**, the **agent,** the **service leaders,** and the **company** itself. Throughout each journey, the customer remained in complete control – but – they engaged in an engineered "flow" from one element to the next which required no additional effort on their part.

The journey was designed to create the best experience for *that* customer, and *that* issue.

It is one thing to be able to offer multiple digital options, **but if the transitions between them are clunky or cumbersome** – if they require the customer to have to "start all over again" every time there is a switch – that creates a much higher-effort experience.

The "Secret Ingredient": OnScreen Voice

One element of Digital Customer Service that may seem subtle at first – but is critically important – is the option of bringing a *verbal conversation* into the *digital experience*.

While migrating *away* from off-screen phone calls is a major goal of digital transformation in service, **OnScreen Voice** is the "secret ingredient" that makes DCS interactions so unique. This is critically important because even in a digital world, there are still many situations in which a customer would benefit from having a verbal conversation.

With OnScreen Communication, the customer can be automatically invited to participate in a voice discussion with an agent from *within* the website, portal, or mobile app, or the customer can enter their number to receive a callback (which still provides the agent with the context of that customer's browsing session in real time).

OnScreen Voice enables the optimal outcome for a live interaction: Enabling the right *agent* to speak with the right *customer* at the right *time*, but without the step of forcing the customer to dial a number and start their journey all over again.

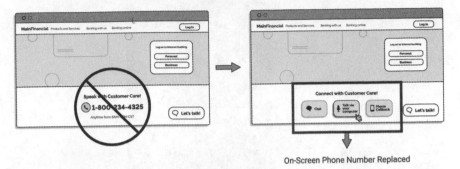

On-Screen Phone Number Replaced

Removing the Phone Number from a Website or App

This illustrates the effect of removing a phone number in an on-screen experience (on the left) and substituting it (on the right) with options for OnScreen Communication. The customer can still engage in a verbal conversation if that would be helpful – but within the website – instead of forcing the customer to start their entire process all over again by having to place a phone call.

While an ever-increasing percentage of customers are now digital-first in their everyday lifestyles, there is (for now) *still* a remaining percentage of customers who *do* choose an off-screen phone call as their entry point.

In DCS, there is still a "bridge" step that can convert even dialed phone calls into on-screen digital experiences.

For Customers with "Dietary Restrictions," Use Near-Screen Voice

While the vast majority of customers enjoy a daily diet of digital experiences, there are still a few who still instinctively pick up the phone when they have a service issue. Just because a customer chooses to initiate an interaction with an off-screen phone call (instead of through a digital entry point) that doesn't mean they are completely out of touch with that company's website or

Real-Life OnScreen Voice Example from Uber

Uber offers customers both an option to dial an off-screen phone call by leaving the app or – a much better option – to press "Free Call" to initiate an OnScreen Voice interaction. The driver receiving the OnScreen call will instantly have all the customer's information because the voice interaction is connected to the app. By contrast, an off-screen call simply passes a Caller ID to the driver with no additional context, so it is much less efficient.

mobile app. If they are calling from a mobile phone, by definition they are *already* on a screen. And even if they are calling from a landline, the majority are somewhere near a laptop, tablet, or desktop computer.[1]

If this is the case, agents should be trained to always ask off-screen phone callers to open the company's website or mobile app – taking the interaction from strictly verbal conversation into a visual experience where the agent can guide and teach the customer how to complete the process (to "show," not to "tell").

The guided nature of a "near-screen" phone call will likely increase that customer's confidence to use self-service next time if this same thing happens again.

The number of off-screen phone calls a company receives should become fewer and fewer in the months and years ahead, but even for those your company is getting, there is almost always a screen nearby to where the customer is calling from. Why not enable agents to bring the visual element of a screen into even those interactions?

The goal should be to provide an option for verbal and visual assistance at the right time in that customer's journey:

- Digital processes can be turned into live assisted interactions (at the right moment) through OnScreen Voice.
- Off-screen interactions can be turned into visual experiences (at the right moment) through near-screen guidance.

So, Do You Still NEED a Phone Number for Customer Service?

This is a provocative topic and has been much-discussed in the service community.

As the number of OnScreen Voice interactions increases, many DCS companies have now discovered that there is no longer the need to display a phone number on the pages of their website or app. If the customer is already online (and often already authenticated), so why would you encourage them to leave, even if they have a need to interact with an agent?

However, there are certain instances where a phone number is still the entry point for some verbal interaction. That said, what if any printed versions of your customer service number were replaced with a QR code that triggers an OnScreen Voice conversation instead? The customer could scan the code, be automatically routed to the right agent and brought to a page on the website where they can collaborate.

Every direct-dialed phone call you get should be considered a missed opportunity to accelerate digital transformation.

> The only times an OnScreen experience may not be possible is if the customer is *driving* or *has their hands full.*

Companies that have transformed service onto a DCS platform have been shifting off-screen phone call volume down significantly (some to as low as now only 10 percent of all customer interactions).

So, how close could your company come to shifting *all* incoming live voice interactions to OnScreen Voice? How long until you really won't NEED a customer service phone number anymore?

Seems like that time is not too far away.

STEP 2: LEARN WHICH DISHES PEOPLE LIKE BEST

When an executive chef creates a new dish, they experiment with different combinations of ingredients to create recipes that people will like, so they can be repeated over and over again. In customer service there are no "experience recipes" per se, but traditionally, customer processes have been diagrammed in a methodological way using **customer journey maps.** Journey mapping is used as an exercise to better understand what customers are experiencing on a step-by-step basis.

While the general principles of this technique have been well-established, the changing psychology and behaviors of customers in the digital-first world require additional inputs not commonly explored with typical journey maps. To transform to DCS, a *different* kind of map is required.

In this next section, we will introduce you to a new way to map how your customers are *thinking and feeling* about various digital self-service processes *as they are experiencing them in real time* on your website or app.

A Note About "Processes"

In order to better understand customer psychology and behavior in self-service interactions, it is helpful to distinguish between a process and an **online session.**

A **process** is best thought of as a single outcome that a customer is trying to achieve – in this case, a single digital self-service interaction. Using the airline industry as an example:

- A *simple* process would be "checking to see if my flight is on time." You click Check Flight Status, put in a flight number (or the To/From cities), and get your response.
- A more *complex* process would be one that requires several steps, but is still oriented toward a single outcome – like changing an existing reservation and checking various flight times and options.

What can be confusing however, is that some online sessions may include multiple processes that should each be handled very differently. DCS provides that kind of flexibility. The trick is to understand which kinds of virtual or live *experiences* match up best with which *processes*.

Digital Self-Serve Inventory (2 × 2)

This is a segmentation chart like others you have seen (sometimes called a four-square), but this one is based on *two subjective dimensions* considered from "inside the mind" of each customer as they are engaging in a specific self-service process.

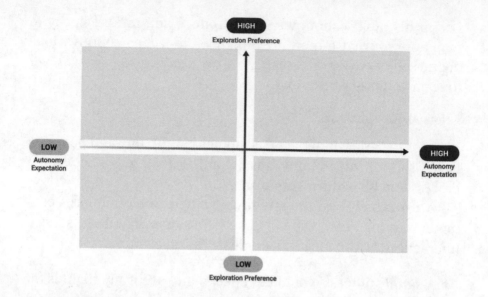

The first consideration (from left to right) is: **Autonomy Expectation (AE).**

[*Customer's thought:* Do I believe I will be able to complete this process on my own?]

- *LOW AE* comes from an assumption that even if the customer wanted to, there is very little likelihood of completing the process without having to interact with a live agent at some point along the way: *"I'm probably going to need some help."*

- *HIGH AE* would be defined by a customer's willingness to and confidence that they are able to accomplish this task on their own: *"I want to, and I know I can."*

(Be careful not to confuse what *you* know about what a customer can or can't do in self-service when resolving specific issues . . . it's not about what's possible, it's about what that person *thinks* is possible in any given situation.)

The second criteria (from top to bottom) is **Exploration Preference (EP).**

[*Customer's thought:* Is this process something I'm enjoying, or is it something I'm trying to "get through and be done with?"]

■ *LOW EP* occurs when a customer has neither the patience, the interest, nor the time to be doing anything but "getting something off their plate."
"I know what I want, just give it to me fast so I can be done already!"

■ *HIGH EP* would be an experience where the customer is enjoying the process of learning more about their choices, is open to comparing options and learning more.
"This is something that is important, and/or something I'm interested in."

If you analyze the most common self-service functions your customers are engaging in on your website or app based on your understanding of *Autonomy Expectation* and *Exploration Preference* (thinking *like* a customer), you will see that almost every self-service function fits into one of just four categories.

Defining the Quadrants

The experiences of engaging in various digital processes can be segmented into one of four categories, based on which of the four squares they would most dominantly fall into. We've assigned names to each of the squares, based on the differences in customer expectations for each of these kinds of processes.

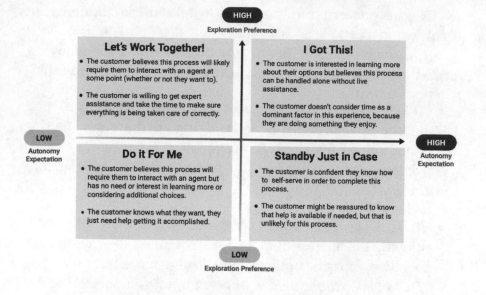

Can you start to see how various processes and issue types would fit into different quadrants on the map? Same *person,* but four different kinds of optimal *experiences* – based on the specific self-service process they're engaged in, measured by two considerations:

- Whether customers think they can complete this process themselves
- Whether they are willing to have an interactive experience

Think about the simplicity of that. All the various processes and all the different experiences customers are having as they're serving themselves – a myriad of combinations – all fall roughly into one of just four categories.

New Ways of Learning About Customer Behavior in Self-Service

The psychology of human behavior in digital self-service is still an emerging science. It is important to remember that across our society, universal access to reliable wifi and the preponderant penetration of smartphone usage is now *just* fully maturing.

As you continue to refine your approach to understanding your customers' taste(s), it will be beneficial to confirm/challenge your assumptions through customer feedback and analysis. There are three approaches companies can use to learn more about the digital behaviors of their customers – the best results will likely come from pursuing all three:

1. Surveys
2. Focus groups
3. Digital body language

To make it a little easier to think *like* your customers, in this section we will share insights and tips that will make it a little easier for you to get a head start on all these "customer learning methods."

Surveys: Suggested Questions

The following could be included in a more detailed "annual relationship survey" or could be conducted as a standalone research project. The goal is to learn more about how various customers think about the experience of engaging in various self-service processes.

*Dear Customer: We want to learn more about how to make it easier for you to access different services and perform various tasks on our website and mobile app. Please consider the following [**X number of**] situations, and for each, rate your response based on these two statements:*

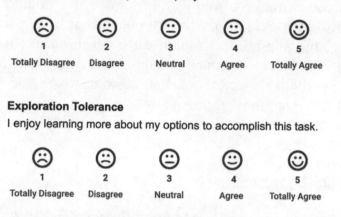

Autonomy Expectation

I expect to complete this process on my own using the website, app or portal provided by the company.

1	2	3	4	5
Totally Disagree	Disagree	Neutral	Agree	Totally Agree

Exploration Tolerance

I enjoy learning more about my options to accomplish this task.

1	2	3	4	5
Totally Disagree	Disagree	Neutral	Agree	Totally Agree

Focus Groups: Suggested Interview Topics

When analyzing the same [X number of] processes as in the above survey, the added benefit to a qualitative approach (during which you can ask follow-up questions) is the opportunity to explore the "feel" side of each customer's experience.

You can learn a lot more about *why* customers have higher and lower degrees of AE and EP for various processes when there is an opportunity to ask second/third-level follow-up questions:

- How does it make you *feel* when you are able to complete a digital process entirely on your own?
- How does it *feel* when you know you can't do something on your own?
- How do you feel when you *think* you can do something on your own, and then as you're doing it, you realize you *can't*?

- How do you feel when you think you *can't* do something on your own, but then learn that you *can,* and that the process was *easier* than you first thought?
- Can you think of any *examples* where that was true – where you learned to do something for the first time on a website?

But in addition to customer research, there are additional insights companies can learn about the digital behaviors of their customers – in real time, as they are interacting with your website or app – by learning to read their body language.

Digital Body Language

Based on the physiology of the human facial structure, each of us has 43 muscles that – through various combinations of contractions – can create over 10,000 unique expressions. Like the one your mom made when she knew you weren't *quite* telling the whole truth about something.

When we are face-to-face with another person, we generally have a pretty good read on what they're thinking, just by looking. Didn't we all learn somewhere that 90 percent of communication is nonverbal?

And even when we're having a *voice* conversation on the phone (while there are fewer cues and clues to consider), there are usually still more than enough to get a "read" on another person – like inflection, word choice, emphasis, tone, VOLUME, etc.

But at the outset of every online interaction, there's only *one* human involved. That person is free to do, and go, and click wherever they want – and no one is there to watch them. So how can you know what they expect from the process, or how they're feeling in the moment? Up until now, most companies wouldn't have any way of knowing – until that customer stopped whatever they were trying to do and dialed the company's phone number.

Determining a customer's expectations about a digital process can be "read" through **digital body language**. These are customer behaviors that include:

- Click/scroll patterns
- Pauses
- Errors
- Form-filling speed/accuracy
- Hovering or stopping locations
- Opening/closing of sections/functions
- Backtracking
- Past history on the site/app

In DCS, it is possible to assess a customer's AE and EP in real time – even as it changes during the course of that interaction:

- As the site asks them questions, how quickly are they responding?
- What choices are they making? (based on product categories, price range, other variables)
- Has this same customer been to this section of your site in the recent past but abandoned their session before they could finish?

Imagine how much easier it would be to design dishes (or customer experiences) that match the right experience to the right customer at the right moment if these clues and cues were all being automatically evaluated in real time.

As you learn more about digital body language, you will continue getting better at knowing exactly what kind of digital service experience to offer a customer at any point in their journey, based on a better understanding of how they are likely *feeling*.

STEP 3: SERVE YOUR BEST DISHES CONSISTENTLY

It should start to become more clear that the best dishes on your service menu will be the ones that match the appropriate OnScreen Enhancements to processes that fit into each quadrant of the Digital Self-Service Inventory.

So, for example, the experience you would want to offer a customer who is engaging in a digital process that falls into the *Let's Work Together* quadrant, would be very different from one who is engaging in a process within the *Standby in Case* quadrant.

Live Assistance vs. Virtual Assistance

Following is a chart that depicts specific OnScreen Enhancements that would likely match up best with processes that fit into each quadrant.

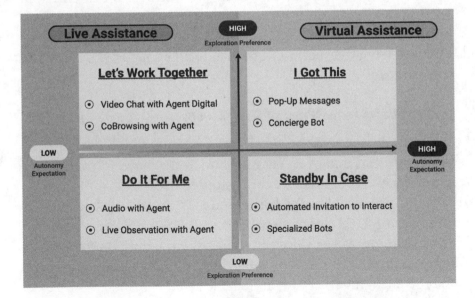

What you can see with a segmentation chart like this is that a person who is engaging in processes that would be positioned on the left side (Let's Work Together and Do It For Me – the low AE side) would likely be better served by an interaction with an agent (**Live Assistance**).

But the processes that are more on the right side (I Got This and Standby in Case – the high AE side) would best be enhanced through automated interactions (**Virtual Assistance**).

Again, very different experiences, engineered through different combinations of OnScreen Enhancements. But in DCS, the system can also determine the relative Autonomy Expectation of each individual customer, throughout each interaction, based on knowable data about that customer.

By detecting exactly where on the 2 × 2 grid a customer is *right now,* OnScreen Automation can be triggered to micro-serve this individual customer in the moment.

And here's another thing worth considering: If a person's Autonomy Expectation *changes* in the midst of an interaction, what then? The flexibility to seamlessly pivot from one OnScreen Enhancement to another is a key feature of DCS that makes it so different from the "bolt-on" approach still being used by so many companies.

Journeys Based on the "Process" Not the "Person"

We all understand the value of *personalization* in digital interactions, but that makes it feel like companies have to cater every experience to every individual customer.

However, what we're learning about the art and science of engineering DCS interactions is that the optimal experience for each customer is based less on their personal digital preferences, and much more on exactly what kind of interaction or process they're engaging in at the moment.

If you were to create a strategy by segmenting customers based on "their digital personae," that might be an interesting thought exercise, but it would likely lead to suboptimal results. Different *processes* feel very different to the same *person.*

EXAMPLE

Let's consider various processes a single customer might experience in their lifetime of interactions with a single company. To illustrate, we'll use a relatable industry: the airline business.

The following chart provides four examples of processes any *one individual customer* might engage in with an airline at some point in their lifetime.

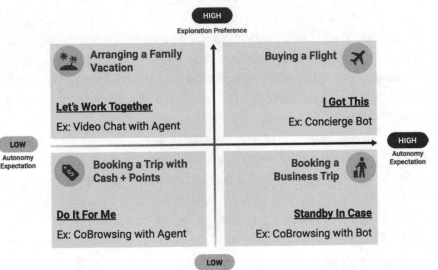

Arranging a Family Vacation

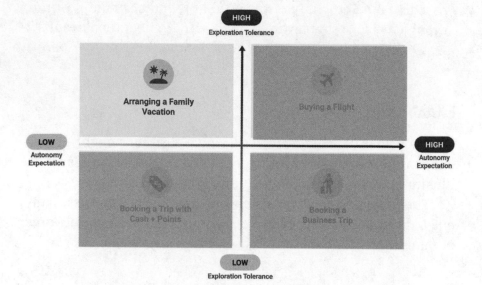

Family vacations are typically fun to plan, but can be complex: Flights, hotels, car rentals, attraction tickets, meal options all have to be arranged, sequenced, and confirmed. That can feel overwhelming. (AE is probably on the lower end of the spectrum, but EP is generally high.)

OnScreen Enhancements: For this process, offering a customer the option of a video chat or an OnScreen Voice interaction with an agent would likely fit that customer's needs at that moment. If they choose to engage, the customer is still in control of the process, but is now being assisted by an expert who is happy to "work together" to create the best outcome for a complex, multi-element process.

Booking a Flight for a Leisure Trip

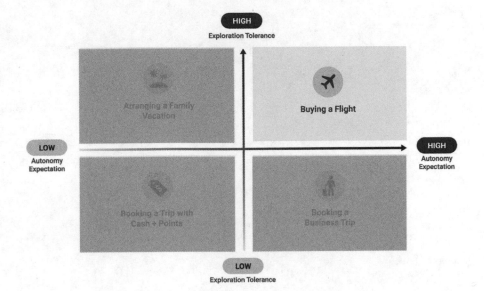

While still a pleasurable experience thinking about the fun you're about to have (high EP) it is a much simpler consideration: Pick your destination, flight times, price, seating assignment – and you're done. Most customers would likely expect they can make their own choices and get through this process on their own (high AE).

OnScreen Enhancements: Imagine if a "concierge" bot popped onto the screen as a customer was beginning the booking process to ask, "Headed to Chicago? Need any help booking your flight?" If the customer clicks "no thanks" (which they will most likely do), they continue in self-service. But they know the option to ask for help is always available – with their choice of chat, voice, or video.

Booking a Multi-destination Trip with Cash and Points

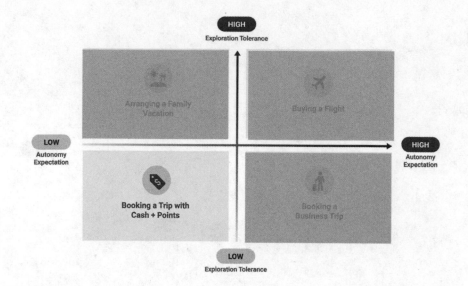

The customer already knows exactly what they want to do (low EP), and likely already has a good idea of what it will cost (dollars and points) but knows that booking a complex itinerary can easily be messed up if they do something wrong. This process is best handled by a professional who can confirm it was all done correctly (low AE).

OnScreen Enhancements: Through Live Observation, as soon as DCS recognizes that this customer is in the midst of a complex process, they should be offered the opportunity to engage in CoBrowsing with an agent, who can "walk them through" the process – ideally teaching them how to do it next time should the need arise.

Booking a Business Trip

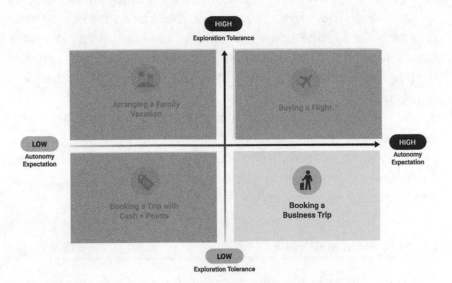

Likely a routine task that the customer has done many times. If they had a "dialogue balloon" above their head it might read, "Just point me in the right direction and I'm good from there."

OnScreen Enhancements: An automatic data-dip could determine if that customer frequently travels to certain cities and use that information to present a prompt asking if they are planning to return to one of those destinations, or if they will be going to a new destination. If so, additional information about that airport/city could then be offered after the booking is complete.

It is tempting to try to generally categorize each customer as more/less "digitally savvy" based on their demographics or past utilization of your digital properties. But the same person who is booking a routine business flight to LaGuardia in New York would likely be operating with a completely different mindset if they were booking a week-long trip to Disney World for a family of five.

As you learn more about your customers and their "taste(s)" based on how they react to various processes, you will continuously improve your ability to dial in the exact recipes that each customer will enjoy best – and be better able to deliver those consistently day-after-day.

EARNING YOUR MICHELIN STARS

The Michelin rating system for restaurants (first introduced in 1926 by the French tire company as a way to encourage motorists to drive out of their way to visit excellent restaurants) is based on three levels of distinction:

- One star is awarded to restaurants that are "*very good* within their category."
- Two stars represent "*excellent* cooking, worth a detour."
- Three stars are reserved for those with "*exceptional* cuisine, worth a special journey."

Transforming to DCS will make your company "exceptional" in the eyes of many customers. If they need help of any kind it happens right on *their* screen – with a seamless transition between virtual and live service. The experience is customer-centric and effortless.

It is now possible to develop a service model in which live inter-actions with an agent will feel like a *value-add* to customers – instead of an added burden.

At a psychological level, people who have a problem or issue just want to feel like they've been heard. Nothing conveys to a customer that you have *heard them* quite like proactively offering help within the context of their interaction, "Hi, Ms. Anderson, I can see you've been thinking about opening an additional account – I can easily help you with that."

The success of DCS comes from creating the right experience for the right customer at the right time, on their terms, not yours. And when *that* happens – when customers feel like you "get" them – why would they ever think about doing business with a competitor?

But this kind of long-term loyalty can only come when you *learn how to learn* about your customers and their digital behaviors – to cater to their taste(s) in order to consistently serve up exceptional experiences on a daily basis.

KEY TAKEAWAYS: CHAPTER 5

- *Start by identifying the right ingredients.* The transformation to a DCS model requires IT considerations that will always be the deciding factor in any "digital" decision process. Your company needs to be confident you have the right platform and partners to bridge the gaps between phone-centric and digital-centric service.

- *Get to know what your customers like.* Your service and digital strategy needs to be built based on continuous improvement and a spirit of restlessness in always trying to think *like* your customers. This is not hard to do, it just requires a different way of listening and learning – through surveys, focus groups, and reading digital body language.

- *Create great dishes that suit your customers taste(s).* Using a combination of live assistance and virtual assistance, DCS experiences can now be engineered to "meet customers where they are" at the entry point of their choice and based on their Autonomy Expectation and Exploration Preference, with OnScreen Enhancements that still keep the customer in total control. Help is always a click away – from an agent who joins you in the middle of *your* interaction.

CHAPTER 6

The People – Empowering Agents, Leaders, and (Even) Bots

What we'll share in this chapter:

- In a digital-first service environment, companies need to empower their people differently – setting them up for greater success by helping them redefine their own roles and to see the overall role of service in a different light.

- The transformation to DCS creates the need for a different talent strategy – who you'll be looking to hire going forward, and for what positions.

- Your "virtual staff" – bots – need to be thought of as "members of the team" as well. They should be hired, trained, and (in some cases) fired just like people, based on how well they learn and contribute to an improved customer experience.

- The best digital experience is often a "hybrid," in which some parts of the experience include virtual assistance by bots and other parts include live assistance by an agent. Carefully curated hybrid journeys benefit the customer, but also make the agent's job much easier and more rewarding.

"I am excited to say that our Employee of the Month is ALSO celebrating his 4th birthday today!

Give it up for Hal!"

FROM CALL CENTER TO CONTACT CENTER TO "COLLABORATION" CENTER

The current operating and staffing model of most contact centers wasn't built for the way customers live today. But transforming to digital-first does NOT mean *people-last*. DCS requires more than just upgrades to systems and software, it is also essential to upgrade the image of the *people* who work in your Digital Customer Service operation.

Some of the most strikingly positive outcomes that develop as companies begin transforming to a digital-first service model go well beyond just the impact on customers. What typically starts to happen within the members of the service team is a transformation of its own. As people begin to internalize the changes they are experiencing in their everyday jobs – as well as getting used to their changing role in the success of the organization – it can feel like the terminology we use to describe the work environment seems out of date. *Again.*

The term *call center* started to fade away a decade or so ago as companies added more and more communication options to the customer service mix – email, chat, and social media – and the name **contact center** became more widely popularized.

> *We don't JUST take calls, because now our customers can contact us through **several different channels**.*

In the DCS environment – *and you can still call it the contact center, or whatever name you want to use* – the *role* itself is less about handling interactions within a given "channel," but much more about being enabled and empowered to **collaborate** with customers in order to help them become more digitally self-sufficient.

Take a moment to think about how that will feel to your people – to enable a customer to do something for themselves – instead of just taking care of problems *for* them. *That's different.*

Transforming to DCS creates an opportunity to upgrade the **role expectations** and **rewards** associated with working in Customer Service.

Is yet *another* name change a requirement for operating in a DCS environment? No. Not if changing the name is just window dressing. But what *is* essential is helping your people see that their roles are transforming – and to help them understand how *they* will benefit as a result.

The Evolution of Role Expectations

In this section we will share stories of service teams that have experienced an **evolution of roles** within three categories:

1. *Agents.* The frontline employees who interact with customers using OnScreen Enhancements.

2. *Leaders.* Executives and managers who are charged with creating the staffing, hiring, and development models within the DCS environment.
3. *Bots.* The AI-powered assistants (some customer-facing and some agent-facing) that provide virtual assistance during an interaction to increase both efficiency and the quality of the experience.

THE AGENTS: RISE OF THE SUPERAGENT

The term being used more frequently over the past few years to describe the frontline role in Customer Service is **superagent.** And again, much like upgrading the image of the contact center to more of a **collaboration center,** this can easily come across as puffery (like referring to a painter as a "liquid recoating specialist" or a Subway employee as a "sandwich artist.").

But the vision of a frontline agent as a superhero is only just a *bit* of a stretch. In DCS, agents are enabled with a host of "powers" they never had before:

- They have access to a *utility belt* of **OnScreen Enhancements** that offer full visual context of the session, and the option to not only "see what the customer is seeing," but to conduct the interaction on the customer's own screen.
- Their "system" surfaces the right customer information at the right time thanks to **agent assistants** (the Robin to their Batman): AI-powered agent-facing bots that suggest responses personalized to the customer they are dealing with and the issue they're trying to resolve at that moment.
- The agent is enabled to focus more personally on the customer, since authentication is taken care of before they join the discussion, and accuracy/compliance issues are automatically monitored. If a concern arises, it is flagged by agent-facing bots in real time throughout the interaction.

In today's world, where the easy issues are almost all resolvable in self-service, being a superagent is essential – because what's being thrown at you is typically *way* harder than before: Customers want more, and they are more demanding – but they also value a great digital experience, especially in situations where an agent is able to work with them right on their screen.

This is the key to how DCS should be introduced to your people – not just why it's a good idea for customers or the company – but rather, what's in it for *me*?

What IS In It For Your Team?

Firsthand experiences among service teams that are well along in their DCS transformation seem to indicate that many of the "bad" parts of being an agent are made a little easier, and almost every "fun" or satisfying part is enabled to occur more frequently:

- *A more effortless agent experience.* Because the virtual assistance offered by agent-facing bots relieves agents of the burden of authentication, retrieving customer information, and compliance issues (which are all being monitored in real time as a "guardrail" against any inadvertent errors), the agent can focus their full attention on creating a better personal experience and connection with that *one person* they are collaborating with.
- *Greater personal satisfaction.* When an agent enters a conversation with a customer, they do so "in the midst of the issue" and on the customer's screen – it is much more of a collaboration or a teaching opportunity instead of a "service interaction." As such, agents are elevated to becoming a *value-add* to each customer's digital experience, instead of just a call center rep churning their way through the phone queue.

Frontline employees of companies that are transforming from a digital-also contact center into a digital-first DCS environment commonly say they are able to "hit home runs" with customers at a much higher rate during interactions that are *partially automated*. The opportunity to create truly *excellent* service interactions becomes more frequent.

When agents enter a customer's journey "where *they* are" (already knowing the context of what that person is looking to accomplish), the number of *rock star moments* in the daily life of an agent is greatly increased from what it would have been in the past.

Joe Borkowicz, chief experience officer for S-3, Shared Service Solutions, says:

Because it's so much easier in DCS to answer a customer or member's need accurately through the use of tools and the digital servicing components, you feel better about this interaction and better about yourself. In the past, those moments where you could really solve a customer's problem and you knew exactly what to do – this came only through experience and repetition. But now, with digital assistance and context, that kind of thing can happen many times a day. The satisfaction is the same – you just get to feel it a lot more frequently.

The result: employees feel like they are being set up for success with a much higher percentage of the customers they interact with.

Members 1st is a local institution in the Harrisburg, Pennsylvania, area. As a family-oriented credit union serving the

Capital area they have a wide member base ranging from IT professionals working in state government, to lifelong eight-decades residents who just got their first iPad last year. Liam Wright is an e-services specialist who has seen a rapid uptick in employee engagement and company pride since they started transforming to a DCS model.

He says many of the agents he has worked with feel like they are helping members do things they would have thought were beyond their ability: "From the CoBrowsing standpoint – once our people help a member see it on their own screen, they know they can do it now, they understand it is *possible*."

He goes on to say, "I think about many members who've told us 'When I called in, I thought that maybe setting up a transfer was impossible. I had no idea how to do it. But now that you've shown how – on my screen – I'm going to give it a try next time.' And after just one interaction like that, we've now established a deeper sense of trust with that member from that moment forward."

What Does the Term Customer Service "Rep" Mean in DCS?

There are many different terms we use to describe frontline service employees – agents, advisors, specialists – of these, the most common is probably customer service representative.

Have you ever taken a moment to think about what that term means? *Rep*? Who are they *representing*?

(*That doesn't even feel like a legitimate question because the answer is obviously: The **company** . . . they are a paid representative of that company, right?*)

True. But what if – during a team huddle – you told all your frontline people:

"From today forward, your job is to represent the *customer* you are interacting with at that one moment. You are being paid *by* the company to represent *them*. To guide them to whatever they need, to teach them how to become more digitally independent, to help them become more self-reliant in an increasingly digital world. *That* is your job from now on."

- *In a **phone-first** service environment, the role is to serve the customer and represent the company.* To take care of their problems and issues. To listen to complaints and try to keep the customer from wanting to churn and go with a competitor. And do it all as efficiently as possible.
- *But in a **digital-first** world, you as an agent are there to represent the customer and serve the company.* The point is to be on the same page as the customer and make them feel like you are on their side. Your job is to empower customers to use the digital tools the company is providing so they can resolve a greater number of future issues on their own.

Even though a contact center might still look like the same with people wearing the same headphones and staring at the same cluster of screens – the role your people play in DCS is very different – more like working in a collaboration center. Not just to serve the customer but to be on the same page with them and guide them along the way.

Another image that will help illustrate how different the agent's role becomes in a DCS environment is "you're something like a Sherpa."

- Your job isn't to tell people *how* to climb Everest, or to make the climb *for* them, you are there to go along and guide *them* throughout the journey. You know the fastest routes, the shortcuts, the dangers to avoid. You're the expert.

■ Of course, when the climber gets back to base camp and eventually home again – the memories and the stories are all about how *they* got to the summit. *But if it wasn't for your wisdom and guidance, it would have been a completely different experience.*

To represent the customer (as an employee of the company) is to signal that you are on that person's side – ready and willing to share your knowledge and expertise on *their* behalf. Your job is not only to resolve issues and take care of problems but to help each customer become smarter.

If that's not a 180 for your people, what is?

Story: AHT vs. THT

Every time I visit with people who work in contact centers and try to "feel" what it's like to do their job, it always bugs me that so many companies still think about AHT. That doesn't seem like the right thing to be measuring.

While AHT was a sufficient metric before customers became so fixated on self-service, in the digital world it is flawed in one important way – it fails to take into account the long-term value of customer *digital self-sufficiency*.

That's why companies should focus almost exclusively on **THT**.

THT is the *total handle time* the company will have to invest in this one customer, from now until (hopefully) forever. The overall cost of operating a service operation isn't based on the average of how long *each interaction* takes, it is based on the total cost of serving each customer throughout their entire *lifetime*.

Total handle time of all customers for the life of your company = Cost of your live service operation

(continued)

The correct strategy going forward should be for each agent to not just resolve this one issue but to help *this customer* become more self-sufficient in the future. Which is why OnScreen Collaboration is so powerful. When used by a skillful agent, it is the ultimate teaching tool.

As the necessity for each individual customer to engage in live interactions declines in the future, so too does their THT. The company's *all-in* cost to serve that customer becomes lower forevermore.

Isn't *that* the way efficiency should be measured in a digital-first world?

—RD

THE LEADERS: RETAINING AND ATTRACTING THE BEST PEOPLE

There are dozens (maybe hundreds) of responsibilities thrust on the shoulders of service leaders – but arguably the most important is building the right team, and setting each person on a path toward success.

Some questions leaders will need to carefully reconsider in the transformation to a DCS environment:

- Who is your company hiring to join your service team, and why are you picking *them*?
- Who are you attracting to even want to *apply* for service jobs in the first place? You can only hire based on who you attract.

If customer service positions are considered lower-paying entry-level jobs, or "easy to get because call centers always have so much turnover," then the types of applicants you attract will likely end up being similar to the same people who have churned out in the past.

But as mentioned in the business case example in Chapter 3, companies that are transforming to DCS are achieving significant cost efficiencies – with reductions in talk time averaging in the 30 percent range. This potentially affords companies the opportunity to increase the pay rate for agents and invest in additional training, while still reducing the overall staff budget.

As the company transforms, so too should the image of frontline service workers. The image of "call center work" as low-paying/high-pressure jobs that cause significant burnout and create constant churn needs an "extreme makeover" that elevates the stature of agents based on their increased capabilities and effectiveness as superagents.

Jeffrey Staw of Open Technology says companies need to think of their agents much more like knowledge workers, instead of "production" employees:

> *That may mean paying somebody more than what we pay them today. I think it will be a job that's harder to get, because different kinds of people will want to work in this environment. Being a service representative is more of a skilled labor job than an unskilled labor job, and I think that that's the way that we need to look at these things to be able to scale in the future.*

If your company were able to offer candidates access to tools and powers that were never available before in typical customer service jobs – how much easier would it be to attract and retain people who will be highly successful in creating excellent digital-first customer interactions? Plus, in a digital operation, agents can be completely productive in a WFH (work-from-home) environment – which means you can expand your recruiting reach to well beyond the geographic confines of a call center environment.

The Hiring Profile of Agents in a DCS Environment

What are the traits required for success as a superagent, and how are they different?

For starters, the **baseline skills** customer service leaders have always prioritized in basic job descriptions still apply:

- Analytic and problem-solving skills
- Comfort working in a fast-paced multitasking environment
- Ability to connect with customers and empathize on a "human" level

But as the role itself transitions from "serving customers" to "joining people on *their* screen to help them become more digitally independent," there are several additional skills that companies should be seeking when making hiring decisions:

- The capability to guide customers through multistep processes
- The flexibility and emotional intelligence to use the right communication and learning style for each individual customer
- An innate sense of knowing how to connect with another person so you are confident they are "getting" what you're showing them

Now, when you look at that list and start thinking about the kinds of *people* who embody that combination of skills and traits – what *other* job comes to mind? *Uhhhh . . . teachers, right?*

Agents = Teachers

Many of the service leaders whose companies have transformed to DCS say they have had great success attracting and hiring people who come from an educational background.

Director of Service Technology Amanda Steinspring at Omaha-based Orion Advisor Solutions says the career switch from the classroom to the DCS environment has been an easy transition for some educators, "We've hired several teachers recently, and they seem to do well. They have been very successful with digital service because they're doing what they know and teaching people how to use the self-serve capabilities we provide."

Jessica Shettel of Members 1st adds:

I operate that way with my employees. I don't give answers. I show you where to find the answer. And that's what our people are doing with the customers they're interacting with – showing them how to do things because that way they don't have to call us back. You know, there's so many times that a member calls in on the phone but they're looking at their computer while they're talking to you. That's a perfect opportunity to teach that person how to work through some process – not to do it for them but to teach them how to do it.

These qualities aren't always immediately apparent on a resume. Yes, if a candidate has a background in teaching or training that's a plus – but there are other ways to assess the potential of a good fit for this evolving role.

Situational interviewing is an excellent way to determine a person's true interpersonal communication style and preferences – asking questions that start with "tell us about a time when . . ." Since candidates are being asked to "tell a story" instead of to "answer an interview question," there is so much more you can learn about that person.

Observations that may be predictive of their ability to be effective in "teaching customers":

■ Are they telling a story from their point of view, or are they bringing the listener "into" their story in a relatable way?

- How well do they describe the setting, the scene? Do you feel like you are "there with them?"
- Are they clarifying *your* knowledge and understanding of the place/situation they're describing? "Have you ever been to [that city]?" or "Have you ever been in [that type of job environment]?"

Sample "Situational Interview" Questions

Basic Skills	Description	Discussion Questions
Analytic and problem-solving skills	As the easier customer issues are now being solved in self-service, agents are confronted with more complex issues more frequently throughout the day. There isn't always a one-size-fits-all approach to every issue. Sometimes agents need to be more creative in developing solutions that will satisfy customers with higher expectations.	■ Give us an example of a time when you ran into an unexpected obstacle during a project. What did you do? ■ Tell us about a time when you were presented with a problem without all the information you needed. How did you handle that situation?

Comfort in multitasking and "active listening" in a fast-paced environment	Agents need to work with customers who have already started the process of resolving their issues – so they have to be comfortable "starting in the middle" instead of beginning every interaction using the same *Square One* call-handling protocol	■ Tell us about a time when you had to do multiple things at once without losing your concentration. ■ When you are very busy, how does that make you feel? ■ What are some ways you've learned to demonstrate to another person that you're truly listening to them?
Degree of excitement about the company and its digital tools	Some companies have discovered that some of their best customers have been successful in becoming their best employees. Who better to interact with than a knowledgeable fan whose passion is palpable?	■ What is it about (this company and its products/services) that you like best? ■ What is it about our service website that you like best? ■ What opportunities can you see that would make it easier for customers to serve themselves?

(continued)

Teaching Skills	Description	Discussion Questions
Passion for helping others become smarter	Whether a candidate has ever worked in an educational environment or not, the likelihood that a person could become a good teacher is best predicted by whether they experience personal satisfaction from sharing new skills and information with others.	■ Tell us about a great teacher you've had in your life. What was so great about them? ■ Tell us about a time when you did something that made someone else feel smarter about something. ■ How did that make *you* feel?
Understanding of varying learning styles	Effective teaching in a digital environment cannot always be accomplished by following a rigid "process map," it requires a DCS agent to connect with each customer in the way that is most comfortable and effective for them – to think *like* the customer.	■ Have you ever thought about the different ways people learn? ■ What could you do differently if you were teaching people with different learning styles?

| "Flexible" personal energy | Part of being able to "meet the customer where they are" is to become sensitive to the degree of confidence different customers have when serving themselves in a digital environment. Agents who are able to "flex" their own style to work best with each individual customer are more likely to be successful in DCS. | ■ What's the difference in the way you personally interact with people in your family who are different ages?
■ Tell us about a time when you had to work together with people who are "different" from you in order to solve a problem. |

The old job of working in a call center or contact center was about "representing the company and solving problems FOR others by following company processes and procedures." But being a **superagent** is more about helping customers to feel smart about *themselves*.

For the right kind of candidate, that feeling is a reward unto itself. *That's* who you should be hiring.

> If you want to run an OK operation, hire people who can *do* the job. But if you want to lead a GREAT operation, you need to attract people who will *love* the job.

Andrea Argueta is the chief operating officer of IDB Global Federal Credit Union in Washington, DC – an early DCS adopter. She says she has witnessed the confidence equity of customers firsthand:

As people experience that live guidance, they're more willing to try something new. And once they've accomplished it and they see that they were able to, then they're more open to repeating it later or even wanting to learn something else. We're giving them the confidence to try even more things on their own. If you set one task for yourself, you accomplish it, you're open to accomplishing even more over time.

Candidates who are most likely to be successful in a DCS environment are those who derive satisfaction and energy from *collaboration and teaching others,* who take pride in helping another person become confident in their own knowledge and more comfortable with new ways of doing things.

THE BOTS: HUMANS AND MACHINES WORKING AS A TEAM

For people who have been in the service industry for years or even decades, the very concept of AI-driven bots interacting directly with customers tends to send a shiver down one's spine.

Here it comes – the singularity – just as we all knew would happen eventually! OK, just tell me, how much severance am I getting?

The pervasive mindset that "the machines are starting to take over" is a very real fear for many people – and if it isn't *acknowledged and addressed* openly, there's the potential for unnecessary negativity or even an inadvertent "sabotage" mentality among some agents.

Here to Help You, Not Replace You

The key to introducing a greater degree of AI into a service operation is to stress that the point isn't to "eliminate human jobs" but to enable agents to do what *agents* do best (assistance in human interactions) and for bots to do what *bots* do best (automating routine processes).

While some bots are designed for customer-facing interactions, the DCS model also includes agent-assistant bots (which are *not* visible to the customer) who provide instant information and suggest "next best actions" that make the job of interacting with customers easier and more effective. Not to tell the agent what to do, but to save time and mental effort, so the agent can focus all of their energy on that customer and their needs.

Bots take care of the up-front work, the repetitive stuff, the drudgery – by automatically surfacing customer data, making suggestions about next best actions and monitoring compliance issues – in order to set each agent up for greater success in consistently creating excellent customer experiences.

The "HR Department" for Your Virtual Team

In a DCS environment, there must be individuals who are in charge of managing both agent- and customer-facing bots (as well as other OnScreen Automation elements).

Bots automate basic inquiries through a conversational user interface – but they should be continuously optimized. They should be thought of similar to an "organic" website interface. You wouldn't release a customer portal and let it sit there for a whole year with no iteration. And while your company likely already has a digital team in charge of improving and optimizing the website, OnScreen Automation also requires an ownership structure with clearly delineated responsibilities.

There are two core positions that companies need to hire for in order to manage their "virtual workforce" and to take the lead in continuous learning as bots improve in effectiveness over time:

- *Automation Designers.* These individuals are in charge of analyzing browsing behavior, agent conversations, and other data to create bots as well as other automated DCS functions.

A great automation designer leverages the context of a conversation and the emotion of the customer to create experiences that are more efficient for customers while reducing cost-to-serve. This includes responsibilities such as chatbot design, personalized notifications/pop-ups for customers, and agent automated assistants.

- *Data Specialists.* They are responsible for collecting and categorizing the data sources that are used by automation designers to create bots, pop-up messages, and invitations for customers to interact with customer service.

Automation designers and data specialists could be sourced by using existing team members (such as former experienced agents) or could be newly hired. These individuals can report to Customer Service with a dotted-line to the digital team, or vice versa. In either case, *these roles create a crucial linkage between the contact center team and the digital team.*

The efficiency gains created by automation rely heavily on **data, context,** and **patterns**. There is a goldmine of each of these buried within customer digital behaviors. Now organizations can fully tap into it through the creativity and technical expertise of automation designers by transforming to a digital-first approach to DCS service.

> *"Genius without education is like silver trapped in a mine."*
> —*Benjamin Franklin*
>
> Without DCS, opportunities for automation are like trapped silver.

Consider the following "flavors" of automation, and see if you can envision how each might be right for certain customers, at certain moments within one interaction:

- *Nonconversational automation.* As a customer navigates the website to complete a transaction, suggestion prompts are presented based on business logic and triggered by specific behaviors in that customer's digital body language.

- *Conversational automation.* A concierge bot can connect the customer to a specialized bot which asks additional questions to clarify the customer's intent. The give-and-take is fully automated, but the "next best action" steps are guided by the customer's responses within a conversational context.

- *Partially automated "hybrid" interactions.* As described in Chapter 5, when the customer's selections or responses in a conversation with a bot leads to a process step where it makes sense to bring in an agent – the invitation is offered to that customer. It is still *their* choice – but if the agent is brought into the discussion, the goal is to proactively enable customer digital self-sufficiency.

Automation should be oriented toward two goals:

- Using bots as "continuous learning tools" to improve the experience for both customers AND agents in ways that are faster and more efficient for all
- Enabling your people to become more human

Through iterative learning, companies can determine which bot interactions are most helpful, and get better at predicting which information should be offered by bots to which customer or which agent at which moment – always looking for every opportunity to automate any process or part of a process – as long as that automation experience is *also* best for the customer.

Personalization, but at scale.

Managing Microbots with Specialized Skill Sets

Much like the sub-pages that branch off the main sections of your website, chatbots should be deployed for distinct, specialized purposes – they should be "use case specific" and they need to be managed based on their ability to be effective within their individual areas of responsibility. This requires automation designers to become something like "the HR department for your virtual agents" – creating hiring, training, and development plans that apply the same basic processes as managing human agents – with some key differences, of course:

- *Hiring.* Bots should be thought of as "Digital SMEs" (subject matter experts) who focus on one process or function, and should be integrated into service interactions based on their exact duties. Many DCS companies have had good success hiring specialized *microbots* that each handle specific use cases: Payment, Account Opening, FAQs, etc.
  It is important to enable coordination of AI engines from multiple vendors, or even home-grown solutions – this ensures bot deployment will evolve as needs and markets continue to evolve.

- *Training.* Bots learn and improve by assimilating data. Yet even the most expertly designed algorithm can't help a bot understand what behaviors are proper or which outcomes are optimal without real-life customer experiences to draw on.
  Leaders need to partner with the service team to ensure bots are getting the right training based on experience in interacting with, teaching, and learning from customers. Service managers should emphasize the desired behaviors they want the bots to develop but data specialists will likely take the lead in areas like:

  - Creating, tagging, and classifying bot responses to improve results
  - Reconfiguring which issues are handled by which bots, and adjusting the triggers that invite a human agent into the discussion

- Setting up training sessions for bots to review and learn from sessions handled by humans

- *Firing.* Companies need to be prepared to "pull the plug" on bots that aren't capable of properly understanding customer needs or are providing incongruous responses. Just as contact center managers must make tough decisions regarding human agents based on performance evaluations, they should also consider when a new bot is worth the investment and when an old bot is ready to retire.

Some of these responsibilities will necessitate a "blending" of what may have once been a division between the service team and the digital team. While there will be some new positions required for success – the economic efficiency of a DCS operation allows the budgetary flexibility to add these positions while still lowering the overall cost of operating the service function.

Much of that efficiency will come as a result of the conversion of customer tasks and self-service processes that can now be completed through OnScreen Enhancements handled in virtual assistance exclusively by bots.

DCS in Action: AI Management Deployment

Profile
- Credit Union serving nearly 500,000 members, with $6+ billion in assets
- Founded in 1930s
- Approx. 1,000 employees

The digitally focused credit union wanted to empower its members to resolve routine online banking tasks on their own

(continued)

by offering virtual assistance options that don't require live help. They also wanted to enable existing contact center staff to handle more complex calls efficiently. It became clear that adding agent and customer-facing chatbots to their DCS solution was the way to solve for both.

But because member experience is always their top priority, whatever they did would have to be simple and include a quick pathway to seamlessly transition from virtual to live service if and when members needed to interact with an agent.

Taking a methodical approach, they diligently analyzed past chat logs to prioritize the most frequent member questions, and partnered with contact center employees to ensure chatbot responses would be on point. They also collaborated with their marketing team to ensure brand consistency while giving the bot a personality, and even a sense of humor, before launching. The CU simultaneously deployed agent-assistant bots to coach agents with editable suggested responses that would feed further optimization.

The new self-service option was well received by members, with now *70+ percent of chatbot interactions* completed autonomously, while others easily and seamlessly transitioned to live help. Each fully automated engagement frees up 5–6 minutes of agent time, enabling them to focus on those members with more complex needs.

As a result, when the Covid-19 pandemic hit and online interactions skyrocketed to more than double, the digital service team was ready and able to handle this record demand using only their existing staff, while increasing the quality of the member experience.

Live Assistance? Virtual Assistance? Or a "Hybrid" of BOTH?

If you were categorizing your entire customer service mix at the broadest level of distinction, one logical way would be to bucket interactions based on "issue types." What are the top *issues* that drive customers to the service portals on your website or app?

Then – remembering back to the Digital Self-Service Inventory from Chapter 5 – imagine dividing these issues into two categories:

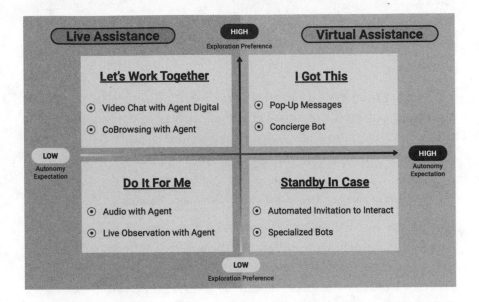

- Issues that would be best handled with **Live Assistance** (the left side of the chart – where the customer likely has a low Autonomy Expectation)
- Other issues that would be more efficiently engineered for **Virtual Assistance** (the right side of the chart – higher Autonomy Expectation)

The assumption might be that the entire resolution journey for any one issue should take place using one form of assistance or the other.

However, in DCS, companies can now begin to engineer "hybrid" digital experiences – in which *some* part of the process is *virtual* via bots and self-service, and *another* part is *handled live* by an agent.

Imagine a sequence of seamless handoffs in a single journey that might look like this:

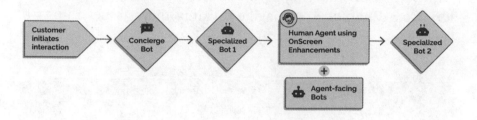

There are many situations where – even though the customer may have gotten onto your website expecting to complete a given process entirely on their own – they would greatly benefit from this kind of hybrid experience.

The Right Mix of Live Assistance and Virtual Assistance Depends on the Process

In DCS, a resolution process doesn't have to be *just* virtual or *just* live anymore. In many ways, the science and art of creating hybrid digital service interactions is the ultimate in "intentionally engineering the experience" so that it feels like lower effort for that customer – which is one of the primary keys to long-term loyalty.

Here are three questions you should be considering that can help identify individual "moments" with a given interaction where toggling back and forth between virtual assistance and live assistance would improve the experience:

1. What could bots do – in advance *of,* or directly *after* a live interaction – to make the agents' job easier and more efficient?
2. Are there situations in which a live agent could walk the customer through *one part* of a process – but *not* all the way to full completion – then enabling the customer to "take over from there"?

3. What are the *right* moments within specific customer journeys in which introducing a live agent into the conversation would create the best possible experience for that customer? That would obviously vary greatly – based on what process or issue the customer has come to your digital domain to engage in.

And because transitioning between virtual assistance and live assistance in DCS is so seamless, service teams should continue to explore each common process with two questions in mind:

- Could we "design" the digital experience for this process so that most customers could complete it using only virtual assistance?
- And if not the entire process, are there parts of the journey that could be handled by virtual assistance – in ways that make the live assistance parts easier for the agent and more effective for the customer?

Compare the Difference in Experience

To see how hybrid experiences improve the quality of the experience for both customers and agents, let's explore one typical customer journey and envision two different service approaches.

EXAMPLE

The company is a retailer with a loyalty program that awards points to customers for each dollar spent, which can then be redeemed for merchandise. A customer (Phil, 52) who has been registered in the loyalty program for the past three years wants to use some of his accumulated points to purchase a set of Bluetooth headphones as a gift for his spouse.

He has never redeemed points before, but his Autonomy Expectation is high at the outset of the interaction.

Scenario 1: "SILOED" SERVICE INTERACTION

- Although Phil instinctively attempts to complete the process in self-service, after a few minutes he loses confidence that he's doing everything correctly and initiates a **chat session** (with a bot).
- The bot is only programmed to help customers who have already done redemptions in the past, so Phil is told he should chat with an agent.
- The agent chat begins and Phil is asked to explain his issue (*again*) and the chat goes on for a minute or two.
- Then the agent realizes that Phil hasn't ever set up an ordering profile – which requires a shift to a *different platform* from where his customer profile is housed.
- That's a *different department*.
- The agent chats to say Phil needs to call the company's 800 number for Customer Service, and puts the number in the chat box.
- Phil makes the call. Then he has to go through the IVR and into the queue. Finally a phone agent comes on, and the entire transaction begins *all over again*.

QUALITY OF EXPERIENCE: Since the journey started online and Phil got part of the way through their order, but then had to abandon the website and start again from the beginning with the agent – *the time spent online was totally wasted* so the process felt frustrating. And while the agent may have been pleasant enough, the process to finally get to resolution likely felt like a *high-effort experience* – one that did not leave Phil feeling "valued" in any way or make him likely to be more loyal to the company in the future.

Scenario 2: DCS "HYBRID" INTERACTION

- A concierge bot asks Phil what he's trying to accomplish, and he responds. The bot takes him directly to the Points Redemption section of the website. As he picks the headphones he wants the bot directs him to the checkout platform but Phil is *unable to process the order*.
- Through "digital body language" DCS detects that he is having an issue and a bot offers the option of connecting with an agent *right on his screen*.
- The agent greets Phil via OnScreen Voice saying, *"Hi, Phil, I'm Sarah. I can see you're trying to use your points to order a set of headphones – I can help you with that."*
- An agent-assistant bot pops up on Sarah's screen (noting that this customer has never redeemed points before), and automatically begins the set-up process. While this is happening behind the scenes, she offers Phil the opportunity to CoBrowse.
- Now Sarah and Phil are looking at Phil's screen *together*.
- Sarah sends Phil an ordering profile (already completed by a bot) which he just needs to e-sign, and shows him how he can order anything he wants with his points.
- Once Phil makes his selection, Sarah guides him to the shipping page, tells Phil how to finish the process, and reminds him he will get a confirmation email within 5–10 minutes.
- Sarah says goodbye, Phil finishes the rest of the transaction *successfully on his own* and the journey ends.

(continued)

QUALITY OF EXPERIENCE: This is an excellent *low-effort* digital experience. Phil started on the company's website, and never had to go anywhere else. When he needed help, it was offered automatically and seamlessly.

When Sarah came into the conversation, she didn't have to ask Phil for any of his personal information, since he was already authenticated in the system, and Sarah was "clued in" by the bots about exactly what Phil needed. She didn't take over the ordering process – Phil was still in total control of his own screen – but they were both "on the same page."

Phil leaves with the satisfaction of knowing he can now complete the redemption process *on his own* any time he likes, and is already excited about what he might want to order next time, after earning more points.

"CONFIDENCE EQUITY" WORKS BOTH WAYS – FOR CUSTOMERS AND AGENTS

As agent-assistant bots, customer-facing concierge bots, and other OnScreen Enhancements are introduced within service interactions, the confidence of customers and agents increases over time – which creates a kind of equity that produces downstream loyalty benefits for *both* groups:

Customers become more likely to continue using self-service functionality once they've been taught how (instead of having the agent do it for them):

- The convenience and agency they experience from becoming more digitally self-sufficient creates a more satisfying experience in the moment.

- This lowers the cost to serve customers in the future, which is a form of equity for the company.

Agents become more confident in two important ways:

- They become smarter and more knowledgeable as agent-assistant bots instantly share the exact information that agent needs at that moment to solve a customer's challenging or more complex issue within the context of the interaction.
- As the number of dissatisfied customer interactions decreases and agents become better at the science and art of "teaching" customers (a skill set that was either unnecessary or under-appreciated in the contact center operating model), their increasing confidence makes the job a more fulfilling and rewarding experience.

AVP and Remote Experience Manager of Portland, Oregon–based Unitus Community Credit Union Char Sears says the transformation to DCS is having a marked impact on the confidence of their agents:

> *We provide our agents with the best tools and resources, which enables them to deliver personalized uplifting service that creates value for each member in every interaction. Teaching skills and techniques are actively utilized, and agents feel a great sense of accomplishment. They are empowered to make recommendations and have the flexibility in guiding our members in those moments. Doing so not only reinforces our Shared Values at Unitus, but builds confidence for our staff and makes them feel like they are on top of the world in their service delivery.*

People *want* to feel good about what they're doing – most employees want to feel like their job contributes to something that matters. This is the very definition of employee engagement – *I see the connection between what I do in my job, and how it connects to something bigger in some way.* For many people in Customer Service, that is what gets them up in the morning and what motivates them to do the best job they can – hour after hour, customer after customer.

The classic "bricklayer story" illustrates this point:

> *A young boy is walking past a construction site where two workers are side-by-side laying bricks to construct a wall. The boy says to the first worker, "Hey Mister, what are you doing?"*
>
> *The guy turns around and barks at the boy (maybe with a cigar in his mouth), "What does it look like I'm doin' kid? I'm layin' bricks."*
>
> *The boy turns to the other man and asks, "What are **you** doing?" The second worker turns with a quiet smile, "I'm helping to build a beautiful new cathedral."*

The "cathedral" in this case is the digital environment your company is engineering – a collaborative operation that will benefit your customers, your company, and the everyday quality of work and life for your *people*.

Story: Standing on the 50-Yard Line

I spent seven years in the airline business with Independence Air, a low-cost carrier operating out of Washington (DC) Dulles International Airport that offered service to 52 cities. We were the fastest-ever start-up in airline history and assembled an amazing service team.

(continued)

For a period of time, Independence Air had the highest customer satisfaction scores in the entire US domestic airline industry (measured by Satmetrix) – higher than United, American, Delta, JetBlue, even Southwest. **90 percent CSAT.** *Crazy high.* That is pretty close to the realistic maximum achievable score in an industry that – as we all know – is notorious for creating unsatisfactory experiences. We were very proud of what we were accomplishing.

One day, as I was finishing a communication workshop with the call center team, a young woman who had only been with the airline for a couple of weeks approached. I'd never met her before but it sure seemed like she might have been crying recently.

She looked up at me with eyes in dire need of a couple of drops of Visine. *"Rick? Why does everybody hate us?"*
WHAT?
My first reaction was to snap back with something like: "What are you, nuts? We have the highest CSAT in the industry. 90 percent! People LOVE us. What are you *talking* about?"

And just before I opened my big fat mouth, I had a "moment" . . . in which I gained an entirely new appreciation for people who interact with customers all day, every day:

- *My* job is to work in an office and get all excited about seeing a number go up.
- *Her* job is to deal mostly with the other 10 percent. That's the world SHE lives in.

– – –

(continued)

Then I had this mental image: "What would 10 percent of our customer base look like . . . if they were all gathered in one place at one time?" (That year we carried over 1 million passengers.)

I pictured her standing on the 50-yard line of a sold-out Michigan Stadium (the largest stadium in the US, located in Ann Arbor, MI) . . . right in the middle of the huge maize-and-blue letter "M" . . . looking up at 100,000 people in the stands . . . every one of them shooting lasers out of their eyeballs aimed right at her.

How does *that* feel . . . to spend all day dealing with people who are frustrated and angry – the 10 percent?

I'd never thought about it that way before. Customer service can be a thankless, emotionally exhausting job that makes you go home feeling like *everyone hates you.*

But it doesn't have to be anymore.

—RD

Consider the positive impact that transforming to a digital-first DCS model will have on your people. When an organization upgrades the role of frontline service from "production workers who serve people" to "knowledge workers who collaborate with our customers," it may *look* like the same job from the outside, but it is a very different and much more rewarding experience on the inside for those who "wear the headset" every day.

KEY TAKEAWAYS: CHAPTER 6

- *It's time for an image makeover in Service.* The strategic emphasis in a contact center is focused on balancing operational efficiency with providing an excellent customer experience. In DCS, the emphasis shifts to helping customers become more digitally self-reliant – which is more efficient *and* creates a better experience for both customers and agents.

- *You need to attract and retain the best talent.* While some of the basic skills of customer service remain the same in DCS, other skills are also important – including an ability to teach effectively. Seek to attract people who get personal satisfaction out of helping others learn. Becoming a digital-first operation also requires the inclusion of new kinds of job categories – like automation designers and data scientists.

- *Start to see your bots as team members.* In a DCS model, bots are an essential part of the workforce and should be hired, trained, celebrated, and fired using the same criteria that have always been applied to human staff development: How well do they learn and improve? What impact are they having on the customer experience?

- *Agents and bots should work together to create "hybrid" experiences.* It is now possible to engineer customer experiences that are partially automated by bots and partially assisted by live agents in a completely seamless way. These hybrid interactions make the agent's job easier and more fulfilling.

CHAPTER 7

The Positioning – How DCS Future-Proofs Your Company

What we'll share in this chapter:

- Transforming to DCS creates the opportunity for companies to *position themselves for future success* – both internally and externally.

- *Internally* – executives and leaders need to send a clear message to the organization that digital transformation is an operational and cultural shift, a change of mindset and a rallying cry that must be continually reinforced in order to position the company for future success.

- *Externally* – a DCS service model creates clear differentiation between your company and competitors. It signals that you are evolving as quickly as your customers have. When service interactions occur on the customer's *own screen* and in front of their eyes, this "experiential differentiation" can be as powerful as product differentiation.

DCS in 2030???

TIME TO MOVE TO THE CENTER OF THE UNIVERSE

Fun facts:

- The Model-T Ford was introduced in 1908. A decade later, approximately 1 in 10 Americans owned a car.[1]
- The iPhone was introduced in 2007. A decade later, approximately three out of four Americans owned a smartphone.[2]

The screen has become the center of our universe. That's not even a "fun fact," it's just a fact of life. So the question your company needs to grapple with is: "Shouldn't the entire service experience take place on the customer's screen?"

Unless you've gone through some really tough times, you've probably never had to live in your car. However, most of us do live on our screens, right?

Unless our society experiences some kind of Luddite revolution in which masses of people suddenly reject technology and start throwing their digital devices onto roaring bonfires in the town square – *this* is the way it's going to be forever more.

Do you ever think about how all that screen-time is impacting us?

Q: Are the digital changes that have happened in our society good or bad? Are we better – as humans – with so many of us heads-down most hours of most days staring at a screen? *Are we?*

A: *There is no right or wrong answer.* There are convincing arguments to be made for "we're much *better* off" *and* "we're way *worse* off." But opinions ultimately don't matter because the world is the way the world is.

But here's a question you *should* answer:

Q: What are you going to *do* about it?

A: Whether you are a primary decision-maker at your company, an influencer of decisions, or just a "bug in the ear" of your superiors – the stance you should be taking is:

From today forward, customer service needs to occur in the center of each customers' universe – *on their screen*.

In this final chapter, we'll explore how to position the transformation to Digital Customer Service (DCS) – in order to build momentum, drive consensus, and increase the impact of the evolution of your service model.

- *Internally:* What is the optimal "message" you should be communicating about digital service? How can you help your people understand why it's so critical for the company, and for them? What do you need your team and your executives to internalize so they will be "leaning in" with you instead of "pushing back?"

- *Externally:* How can you position the "experience" customers have in DCS interactions as an advantage over competitors? If CX is a true differentiator, how can DCS make customers feel smarter about doing business with your company, and most importantly, about *themselves*? And how will that kind of reaction help to future-proof your business?

INTERNALLY: IT'S A 6 × 3 AND A-TO-Z WORLD

Those automatons who sing all day in the Fantasyland section of Walt Disney World have never been more correct: For most of us who live on our screens all day, it *is* a small world after all – approximately *6 inches tall by 3 inches wide.*

No matter how obvious this is just from our own personal observations *(raise your hand if there is some screen within one yard of where you are right now . . . yeah, that's all of us),* at many companies it still doesn't feel like the message has fully sunk in.

As quickly as digital technology and smartphone ubiquity have evolved – enabling each of us to have access to anything and everything we could ever need or want, all within the palm of one's hand – most companies are only just now coming to the realization that they have not transformed nearly as fast as their customers.

This is why the message that "we must live on **our customer's screens**" is more critical than ever. To the extent that your company is still receiving thousands or even millions of phone calls per year, that's a signal that your company is no longer in touch with the way the world works. That's not how customers live.

They want to be in control at all times, and the screen is the center of their universe. The most "high-effort" parts of any customer experience come from the feeling that the *company* is in total control, and I'm *not.*

ICMI founding partner Brad Cleveland says companies need to come to the realization that most customers have become almost entirely digitally oriented so quickly. "There are so many things customers want to do by themselves now. The desire for low-touch, or even no-touch experiences was high before and has only grown since the pandemic." He says, "Customers get upset 'when I can't do what I want to do, the way I want to do it' and that isn't likely to change."

Justin Robbins asserts that many organizations are still awakening to the fact that customers are hungry for digital experiences that take place on their screen:

> *I think a lot of companies are doing the opposite of digital transformation, they're just trying to avoid digital stagnation, meaning they don't want the tools and systems they're using to become obsolete or ineffective. To me, transformation has got to be based on a very clear definition of the overall digital strategy for the business – what you're hoping to enable, what problems you're trying to solve, what's the value you're trying to drive, what kind of experience are you trying to create for your customers?*

Digital transformation in customer service may have seemed like a "tomorrow" consideration for many companies just a few years ago, but it is quickly becoming a matter of "right now" urgency as more customers are on their screens most hours of the day, and have now experienced service interactions with companies that were founded as digital natives.

John Goodman, the author of the National Rage Study mentioned in Chapter 1, says all you have to do is consider your own personal experiences with the "digital super-companies" that now dominate the landscape – often referred to as the **A-to-Z phenomenon**: "A small number of companies have completely re-invented what great service feels like – and as always, Amazon and Zappos are the most frequently mentioned – but that kind of experience has now become the new standard, while the average company is perceived as having done a worse job."

In order for your company to fully "get onboard" with a commitment to transforming your service operation, the core message that needs to be socialized, popularized, and internalized up and down the org chart is:

> "We can't claim to be customer-centric if so many customers are still calling us on the phone! We are now living in a 6 × 3 and A-to-Z world. To succeed, to compete and to stay ahead, we've *got* to evolve as fast as our customers already have."

Why Customer Service for "Traditional" Companies – Like Casino Blackjack – Isn't Fair

Have you ever played blackjack? You know, each player gets two cards and the dealer gets two cards. From there, both sides can either stand pat with the total they have or keep drawing more cards. Closest to 21 wins. But be careful, because if you go over 21, *you lose*. So simple.

You, as the player, are free to make your own choices for every hand. You can stand on 9 if you feel like it, or you can take a hit on 19 *(please don't do either of those things, ever!)*. But your decisions are entirely your own.

The dealer, however, has to play by rigid "house rules." Dealers must take a *hit* if their total is 16 or less, and they must *stand* if it is 17 or higher. That basic set of rules is how blackjack is played everywhere from Vegas to Monte Carlo to your kitchen table.

But here's the thing: You, as the bettor, can play by the same exact rules as the dealer – and in most cases you *should*.

So why does the house win so much money? If you're drawing from the same deck and playing by the same rules, shouldn't it be a 50/50 game? Shouldn't the players and the house come out dead even every time?

But the house has one *clever advantage* that most players never even notice.

- If you *tie* the dealer – if you both have 20, for example – that's a "push" and you get your bet back. No one loses.
- Of course, if you draw one card too many and "bust" by going over 21, your wager is swept away on the spot.
- However, in that same hand – if the dealer ALSO busts, they don't reach back into the chip rack, refund your bet apologetically, and offer you a free drink. *You already lost.*

The house's advantage is that *they get to go last.*

This is why the companies that invented themselves *as* digital companies (the A-to-Z companies) have such a leg up. They were conceived based on the way people think and behave in today's digital world. *They got to go last.*

But service organizations founded 15 or more years ago (let alone 50 years ago) are now faced with having to compete in the digital arena – to somehow emulate an "Amazon-like" experience. Being a "traditional" organization can feel like a massive disadvantage – and no matter how much these companies have tried to evolve, it seems nearly impossible to keep up.

However, thanks to a convergence of technology, creativity, and a deeper understanding of customer digital psychology, the opportunity to transform to a seamless, effortless, economically efficient DCS operation is available to virtually *every* company. It is in many ways the ultimate do-over. Your organization needs to recognize that now is the time to take the steps necessary to *reinvent* the way you serve your customers.

In a 6 × 3 and A-to-Z world, customers are on screen with friends, family and colleagues all day. They prefer this digital lifestyle because it gives them control (convenience and agency). If your company isn't positioned in a way that feels "in sync" with this behavioral evolution of digital-first customers, it is easier than ever for them to switch to another competitor.

Transitioning to DCS *positions* you in a way that is more consistent with how people live in today's world. This will help you meet and exceed the "expectation" for how service is *supposed* to feel – an expectation set by digitally native companies like Amazon and Zappos (which, of course are now the same company!).

The Dichotomy of Expectations

For all the talk over the past few years about the continual rise in **customer expectations**, one thing that's become increasingly apparent is the *sloppiness* of the term itself. A quick count shows we've already used the words "customer expectations" 12 times so far to this point in this book (including twice in just THIS paragraph!), but it feels like those two words should have an **(*)** next to them. What we've been observing is that at a *psychological level* there are *two sets* of customer expectations that most people experience (simultaneously!) just as they are initiating a service interaction – and they are polar opposites.

- *Customers expect digital service experiences to be excellent.* They have a standard that they think is reasonable, and they don't think they should have to settle for less than that.
- *Customers also expect that their service interaction will be a big hassle.* They anticipate that their standard will not be met.

They expect service interactions to be increasingly digital, customized, and personalized. And why shouldn't they? Most people believe companies have all the information about them somewhere in their "systems" – what they've purchased, how much they've spent, how long they've been buying from the company, their overall satisfaction with the company through whatever feedback they've ever provided in surveys – so there's an expectation that every interaction should be "all about *me*."

However, we also know – based on qualitative customer research from focus groups and interviews – that when a problem arises and there's a need to reach out to customer service, they are often disappointed:

This leads to this potentially dizzying dissonance:

I expect this interaction will be amazing, *and* I also expect it to be a huge pain.

- So, was it excellent because it was exactly what I expected?
- Or was it terrible because it was exactly what I expected?

Change the Experience, Shift the Mindset

You need to engineer the experiences your customers are having in a way that makes them feel "digitally effortless."

Consider the following: How differently would customers feel if you were creating a service interaction that put *them* totally in charge – because it was happening on *their* screen – but you still offered the opportunity to connect with an agent at any time they feel the need, but without ever having to dial a phone number ever again? How would that impact their "confidence equity" over time?

Digital transformation in service is the key to long-term customer loyalty. Loyalty is the key to your long-term success – and it mostly comes from how customers feel about us. And by understanding the psychology of digital interactions more clearly – focusing a little more attention and communication on how customers feel – think about how your company could position its service experience in a way that makes customers feel better about doing business with you.

To the degree that your influence can reach – this is the *mindset shift* you need to be part of engineering in your organization:

As an organization, we now have the opportunity to influence the way customers feel about doing business with us in ways that were never available before – the technology now exists – and it's not only way better for customers but it's far more efficient than what we've been doing.

Story: The Ultimate "Effortless Experience"

The first discovery of the impact of "customer effort" on long-term loyalty – the subject of *The Effortless Experience*[3] – was sparked by a research project that sought to answer one single, simple question:

What is the best predictor of a customer's future loyalty behavior right AFTER they have just engaged in a service interaction?

What we learned is that a customer's answer to this one question: "How much effort was required for you to get your issue resolved?" was more predictive of that person's future behavior than *any other question* we tested.

- Way more accurate than "How satisfied were you?"
- Even somewhat more than "How likely are you to recommend us?"

And – at first – I assumed that reducing "effort" was mostly based on **exertion,** or what customers have to *do* during the span of an overall service interaction:

- How many things they have to *do*
- How hard it is to *do* those things
- How long it takes to *do* those things

(continued)

Even if you didn't take physics, the whole idea of: *"Exertion = The amount of energy required to push one kilo of weight over a distance of one meter"* seems like something we probably all learned at some point. And virtually every company that first heard of the idea of measuring customer effort could immediately identify a few quick-fixes in the area of process simplification, which had a measurable impact on effort and loyalty. We were excited to learn more.

About a year later, we did a follow-on study to better understand exactly *how* customers perceive "effort" in service interactions:

- What thoughts were being triggered in their minds?
- What do they even mean by *effort* (in our testing, it was never defined in any way other than using the word).

What we discovered became the single biggest "light bulb moment" I experienced in all our research. Maybe ever. Effort is perceived *way* differently than I had first thought.

In the minds of customers, their *exertion* accounted for exactly 34.6 percent of how they experience effort: The number of *things* they have to do, the *time* it takes, the *difficulty* of doing certain things – those things matter, to an extent.

But the surprising discovery was that the vast majority of how people experience "effort" – the other 65.4 percent – is based on their subjective impression of how they *felt* during the interaction.

- Is the company making it easier or more difficult to get this problem solved?
- If I'm dealing with an agent, are they on *my* side or are they just reading a script and regurgitating company policy?

(continued)

- Are they taking my personal needs and situation into account?
- Are they making me feel "valued"?

Bottom Line: Customer Effort Is One-Third Do, but Two-Thirds Feel.

And from that, we spent many years helping companies work on the "feel" side of reducing effort – because for the most part, there was only *so much* companies could do to change the "do" parts of working within a traditional phone-centric service model.

But now there *is* something companies can do.

The biggest thing I've been learning about digital transformation in customer service is that it is the solution to both the *do* and the *feel* sides of customer effort.

In a DCS model, the number of things customers have to *do* (and more importantly, the things they don't ever have to re-*do*) are greatly simplified.

But the way the experience *feels* is different, too.

In an on-screen world, that's the hallmark of a low-effort experience.

—RD

EXAMPLE

With OnScreen Collaboration – an agent in DCS can start a conversation four steps ahead. Speaking with someone who can anticipate what you're trying to do without having to ask, who's showing you how to do things more easily yourself – that makes you feel smarter. And more valued. Like a VIP. Like, "This company gets me." That's using technology to enable agents to create a very different experience.

When we first wrote *The Effortless Experience*, the smartest option for companies was to use our understanding of customer psychology to "engineer" customer experiences so that they would feel like less effort.

Now, with DCS, it is possible to change both the *do* and the *feel* sides of service *simultaneously*.

EXTERNALLY: CX IS THE LAST FRONTIER FOR DIFFERENTIATION

How *different* is your company or organization from your competitors?

That is an important question, but it's unfair to ask YOU – because *you know too much*. If you're a service leader, a CX professional, or any part of your company's digital team, you are being paid to analyze (perhaps even micro-analyze) the complexities and idiosyncrasies of the marketplace your organization competes in. And you likely have been doing so for years.

You have what's called *the curse of knowledge*.

But even your most loyal customers who've been with you for years or decades are unlikely to have even a fraction of your understanding about the difference between what your company offers and what other similar companies are offering.

No matter how much daylight you believe there is between your company and your competitors, the gap appears much smaller among people who don't have your years of experience.

Products and even services have become so overcommoditized. Among competitors, the degree of copy-cat-ism is typically very high. The minute you come up with something that feels very different – if it's any good – others in your category will likely adopt it almost immediately.

Take a common competitive set that most of us are generally familiar with – national pizza delivery chains:

How *different* is Pizza Hut from Domino's from Papa John's?

- Yes, you may like one of those brands better.
- You may prefer the crust, sauce, cheese or toppings that one offers compared to others.
- One of them may be offering a special at the moment that could save you a few dollars.

But aren't they essentially the same types of companies, doing virtually the same exact things?

This is why **customer experience** is the final frontier in competitiveness and differentiation. It is your last best hope to *position your organization differently* from others who offer more or less the same thing, in the minds of people who don't know a fraction of what you know. The choice you make about which pizza delivery company to order from will likely be based as much on the delivery experience as it is on the pizza itself.

So, what is *your* company doing to create a *truly* different experience?

Positioning "Digital CX" as a Differentiator

To digital-first customers, your website is your "virtual presence." It is *your* brand, but it plays out on your *customer's* screen. This is the arena where differentiation takes place. In the mall called The Cloud, it is your storefront. But the opportunity to truly differentiate lies not just within the visual elements of design and graphics, but also based on the digital experience your customers are having every day with your company.

Customer service expert Shep Hyken says creating a digital experience that makes things as easy and convenient as possible is a differentiator that makes economic sense, "You don't have to sacrifice profit to create additional convenience, customers are willing to pay more – it's become normal. He says that 62 percent of customers are willing to pay more for better service and 69 percent are willing to pay more for greater convenience. Price is kind of important, but if you can make my life easier, save me time and a big hassle, that used to be a luxury – but today that's considered standard equipment."

Jacqueline M. Ridley is a customer alignment strategist whose firm Break Tradition has worked with dozens of companies to help them better understand the psychological impact of the customer experience. She says it is not enough to emphasize what is different or better about your company at a logical level, you must also understand the differences at an emotional level: "When a customer makes a purchase, something drove them to your company, but are they walking away feeling like they want to tell people about the experience? Is the experience fulfilling a psychological need of some kind?"

She goes on to say that since customers have unlimited access to information about your company and your competitors – including feedback and reviews from peers – creating a differentiated experience is crucial:

> *Customers are savvy, they've done their research, they know there are other companies that do the same things. They want to feel like they're "part of the family" and they want to know they're being heard and that someone is listening. That is the kind of experience that makes one company*

different from another. But when customers have a problem that seems hard to solve or creates a lot of negative mental energy, it's like letting someone down in an intimate relationship. That takes a psychological toll.

To customers, what's *different* about a DCS experience is that it's easy. It's effortless. It is the ultimate in convenience because whatever I need is right there on my screen.

DCS in Action: Differentiating Service for International Customers

Profile:

- International banking provider
- Serving customers who frequently travel between the US and 75 countries across North America, Latin America, and Europe

This organization had traditionally supported customers from a single physical branch at their global headquarters location, as well as a call center operation. They also offered basic online functionality.

But as customers became more digitally self-sufficient, demand grew for enhanced online options that would enable a secure but personalized experience regardless of their location.

The organization chose to implement a DCS solution that included video, chat, OnScreen Voice, and CoBrowsing.

With DCS now fully operational, customers simply log on to the website or the banking application and connect directly with the banking team.

(continued)

Inquiries are intelligently routed to the right agent at the right time with agents pivoting proactively to support customers through video or OnScreen Voice:

- *Efficiency improvements.* Service leaders report the DCS solution has been easy to administer, and agents were onboarded with less than a half-day of training. The bank has an impressive average of only 6 seconds of wait time for digital engagements.
- *Experience improvements.* Customer satisfaction is significantly improved across-the-board. A recent customer survey revealed that 79 percent of respondents were satisfied or very satisfied with their digital banking experience. The expense of international calling is now eliminated as live interactions are now free for customers who connect with OnScreen Voice over their wifi or data plan.

Since interactions are no longer defined by physical location and service representatives are only a click away, the customer experience is now consistently excellent whether the client is at home walking up to a teller window, or traveling through the African desert or the rainforests of Latin America.

You Must Accelerate Your Transformation Just to Keep Pace

The massive changes in customer expectations and behaviors within digital self-service we've all been witness to – from zero expectation, to the expectation that *everything should happen on my screen with me in total control* – have now gone to a point that is edging toward its realistic maximum.

Think about how quickly that happened. If you take "one giant step back" and consider the "evolution" of digital self-service – from 1977 (the first ATMs), to today's all-digital world – that transition occurred in about a second-and-a-half in evolutionary terms.

So, it doesn't seem fair to expect that "traditional" companies should be able to transform their service operations as quickly as *that*.

Perhaps customers should "cut a break" to those companies and organizations that have been a little slower in their digital transformation. Or, for companies that have evolved their digital capability in some other areas, but haven't quite reinvented the way they serve customers.

Maybe customers should be more patient and forgiving. But that's not how it works.

Joe Borkowicz of Shared Service Solutions says:

You have to evolve to stay relevant, right? I believe to stay relevant in today's marketplace – this is either with your customer set, your member set or your employee set – you have to embrace digital capabilities. If not, you're gonna be left out. It's about relevance. And because in almost every marketplace, there's someone trying to steal your share. There's too many disruptors.

If the way customers perceive the experience of doing business with you feels out of date, or *less digitally evolved* than they have become, that is *not* the position you want to be in.

Using DCS Technology to Create a Differentiated "Human" Experience

What do you and your company want to be known for? What do you value most? Every organization has a set of **values** – maybe they're posted on the walls of break rooms or perhaps they're framed and on display in a lobby or waiting area.

Take a look at them (most companies have about three to five) – and consider the following distinction between them:

- How many of your values are about being a great *organization*?
- How many of your values are about being great *people*?

At most companies, values tend to skew slightly toward the "great people" side. Honesty. Integrity. Fairness. Passion. Equality. Leadership. Empathy.

Any of those on your list? Probably.

So how *do* you want customers to be thinking about your company? How are you projecting your "values" in a way that would make a customer be more loyal? Especially following a service interaction, in which they are likely at the greatest risk of disloyalty if it goes poorly.

What "values" should you be portraying in the way you interact with customers?

In a digital-first world, even during digital interactions that are completely automated – the experience should still feel "human." That doesn't mean chipper, cheerful, and friendly (no customer is going to buy it when a bot tries to fake being "bubbly"). But the experience should feel like it is empowering to customers, it should make them feel that they are in charge, and that your goal as a company (that they chose to do business with) is to make it easier for them to become more digitally self-sufficient.

As a solutions architect working in a DCS environment, Mark Coleman of Members 1st says he's proud of the fact that his company is a technology leader in their space, because of the *human* experience it creates:

> *So, I think the approach that we have – connecting people with people – allows them to understand that it's more than just technology. It is more, there's people behind this. There's people behind everything. It's not just the machines building the system, the code, the interactions. At some point there is a person involved and trying to get that one person on our side as close as we can to the one person on the other side through digital means is the goal for how we want people to see us.*

For your company to achieve competitive success in the months and years ahead, now is the time for you to use your creativity and expertise to influence the three most critical factors in any transformation:

- Process
- People
- Positioning

Transforming to a digital-first DCS service model improves all areas of the business and culture of a company – fundamentally changing how the organization operates and delivers value to customers.

We hope that what we've shared in this final section – and throughout the chapters of this book – will give you the greatest possible head start in the direction of a successful and rewarding digital transformation.

KEY TAKEAWAYS: CHAPTER 7

- *The screen is the center of the universe.* People of all ages now live on their screens. Whether you like it or not, whether it's better for society or not – *that's just the way we've evolved.* Companies need to do the same. The customer's screen needs to become the single focal point for all interactions. It's a 6 × 3 world.

- *The "digital disadvantage" can be overcome.* For "traditional" companies, the pressure to create an experience that competes with companies like Amazon and Zappos seemed insurmountable. That is no longer true. Transforming to DCS is being accomplished by companies of all sizes, even smaller organizations that have served their local regions for the past century.

- *DCS is the last best hope for differentiation.* In a commoditized industry or segment, creating a truly different customer experience is often the best way to create separation between you and your competitors. An effortless, seamless, personalized DCS service experience feels different at an emotional level. For many customers it is more self-affirming, which promotes greater long-term loyalty.

Epilogue: To Infinity and Beyond

If you've come this far, we hope we've given you a lot to think about. And *since* you've come this far, here's one *more* thing to think about:

WHY DID YOU GET INTO THIS BUSINESS?

Whatever your exact title – if your job has anything to do with the experience of your customers – you do this for a reason. You probably could have chosen to do something else with your career. But when you use your skills and expertise to create a great experience for your customers, *how does that make you feel?*

Yes, this profession is harder than others. There are always a million issues to deal with and brush fires to extinguish. It can be an all-consuming 24/7/365 lifestyle. So perhaps you don't spend enough time reflecting on *why* you do this.

But if you take a moment, we hope you can start to see what we've been seeing in our research: *Whatever it is you love about serving customers* can now be experienced at a whole new level.

The world has transformed. And now . . . it's our turn. The digital transformation of customer service is no longer a thing of the future. And even if you're not a massive global organization, the benefits are equally available to just about every company.

Your company needs to make a choice about whether you're going to lean into "the way the world is going" – or hang in there for a few more years trying to milk the last drops out of a service model that is starting to look as out-of-touch as showing up for a first date wearing a pair of Hammer pants or a tube top.

Transformation can be scary. We hear you. The easiest decision is to *not* decide, and just keep doing things the way you've been doing.

So here's one final thing to think about: Do you remember the first time you saw *Toy Story*? It was released on November 22, 1995. You may recall that Thanksgiving weekend as the "coming out party" for the **digital transformation of animated features**. That was the first time we ever saw a full-length movie that came spitting out of a hard drive.

Pixar is a technology company that was founded with one core mission: *Tell great stories*. And what they learned is that digital transformation enabled them to accomplish that goal in ways that had always been limited by the confines of ink-and-pen on celluloid.

The job of telling great stories never changed. But technology made it possible to tell stories that could never be told before. *Like what happens inside the toy box when no one's home.*

Can you see how the digital transformation of customer service is the opportunity for *you* to tell the story *you've* wanted to tell for years? The story about how your company really cares about its customers, and that you value them. That you are willing to evolve as quickly as they have, and to create a digital experience that is seamless and effortless so they will always remain loyal.

The advent of DCS and the adoption of a "digital-first" mindset creates an opportunity for you to refocus on the things you love about serving customers: Creating a great experience. Helping people solve problems. Making others feel smarter about themselves.

But now it's possible to do these things in an even more profound and "magical" way – by meeting your customers where *they* are:

- In their entry point of choice
- In the midst of the interaction they already started online
- And, in the midst of their own transition to becoming digital-first people

Don't let your company be held back by the peaks and valleys of the past. Digital transformation enables you to fall in love all over again with the feeling of creating a great experience for others. To do what *you* do best – only now, in ways that will be even better.

For your customers, for your company, for your team, and for yourself.

By the way: Six days after the release of *Toy Story* – on November 28, 1995 – Pixar went public.

It would end up as the largest IPO of that year. *Just sayin'*.

—RD and DM

Digital Customer Service FAQs

CAN A BUSINESS WITH LIMITED DIGITAL SELF-SERVICE TRANSFORM TO DCS?

If digital self-serve is limited and online experiences are more informational (the customer simply visits the website or mobile app to learn more but can't do much other than read or watch content), then the value of DCS will depend largely on the volume of customers that engage in these digital experiences. When traffic is substantial, DCS is still very valuable. It empowers the business to serve customers where they are (in their primary entry point). All that said, if the business has no digital presence, then DCS will be limited to powering a Messaging / Social approach (SMS, Apple Business Chat, WhatsApp, etc.).

Robust digital self-serve experiences greatly amplify the OnScreen Enhancements that an organization provides. When customers have the opportunity to complete processes online, DCS introduces virtual or live assistance right at the point of need. The customer is on the website, portal, or app working through an issue, and a bot or agent can jump right into the process with context. This creates a much lower-effort experience for customers and contributes to greater customer loyalty.

HOW WILL DCS OPERATE IF OUR COMPANY HAS AN EXISTING CRM PLATFORM?

When we consider how DCS fits with CRM systems (customer relationship management), the same logic applies to any *system of record* (such as a policy admin or ERP platform). DCS acts as a nimble layer on top of any information source or database by integrating and surfacing the right information and exporting it back – in some cases to an agent, and in others directly to the customer. Since many organizations have systems of record in place already, they prefer to layer DCS on top of those systems as a *system of interaction.*

For example, in an OnScreen Voice interaction, the DCS platform could analyze the conversation, detect that the customer has made a similar purchase in the past, and surface information from the CRM about that specific transaction to the agent. Once the interaction is over, the transcript of the conversation is exported back to the CRM. Instead of the agent digging through the CRM to find the details needed for the customer, DCS provides an intelligence layer to retrieve and export the information that is necessary.

It is worth noting that some CRM systems offer certain elements of DCS natively or are partners with DCS vendors to offer some OnScreen Enhancements. However, it tends to be far more effective to specialize DCS within its own interface because CRM systems are not optimized as systems of interaction.

HOW DO CHATBOTS FIT IN WITH DCS?

Chatbots (both agent-assistant as well as the customer-facing bots) are a fundamental part of OnScreen Automation within DCS. As described throughout the book, DCS is not about offering every possible digital channel. It is assembling the necessary ingredients and then determining "which dishes to cook" (or in this case, which customer journeys) based on customer preferences in any given process (as determined by the degree of Exploration Preference and Autonomy Expectation).

Some organizations may have digital processes that are better suited for virtual assistance, some may opt for primarily live assistance – or (as described in Chapter 5) "hybrid" interactions. The most important consideration for the deployment of chatbots (or any form of OnScreen Automation, Collaboration, and Communication) is that bots must fit seamlessly into the other DCS elements that the company provides.

HOW DOES AN EXISTING KNOWLEDGE BASE FIT IN WITH DCS?

Much like CRM, knowledge bases (KBs) are systems that hold information about the business and its products/services. Sometimes, a knowledge base can be a part of a DCS platform and other times organizations have already invested in these systems independently. Much like with an existing CRM system, DCS acts as a nimble layer on top of any existing information source by integrating, surfacing, and exporting the right information at the right time.

For example, an agent is interacting with a customer about an issue with a change of address request and the knowledge base entry is automatically "popped up" to the agent for their reference.

It is worth noting that the most advanced DCS organizations are rebuilding their KBs using chatbots. The reason for this is that KBs are traditionally long-form and static content. However, chatbots are short-form, conversational, and dynamic – making the experience of accessing support information more effortless for customers and agents.

HOW DOES AN SMS/MESSAGING FOCUSED STRATEGY FIT IN WITH DCS?

SMS and messaging are increasingly popular with consumers and are important elements of the OnScreen Communication offerings within DCS. When a business has several digital processes in which customers have high Autonomy Expectation, then SMS and messaging are critical. They allow the customer to request quick assistance while still continuing with their preference to self-serve. These communication options are also especially important when interaction efficiency is the primary key performance indicator (KPI). They allow for multiple interactions to take place at the same time and to continue conversations where they left off, in an asynchronous way at a customer's convenience.

HOW IS DCS DIFFERENT FOR SPECIFIC INDUSTRIES?

DCS is a universal approach regardless of industries (including B2Cs, B2Bs, and hybrids). The main variable is the maturity of digital transformation at each company to date, which tends to vary based on industry. Companies are either digitally "native" or digitally "migrant," but DCS can lower operating costs and improve customer experience in either case.

For instance, an e-commerce retailer that was established in the last 10–20 years will most likely have a much higher degree of transformation maturity than a brick-and-mortar retailer established in the 1950s. Digitally native organizations tend to operate most processes with the assumption that the majority of customers have high Autonomy Expectation so their DCS approach leans toward virtual instead of live assistance. But since DCS can be activated in a variety of ways that accommodate any industry or company, it can create the same kind of success with any customer base.

HOW DOES DCS WORK IN A "MOBILE" ENVIRONMENT?

DCS is completely device independent. If there is a screen the customer is using to visit your company in any way, OnScreen Enhancements can and should be offered. As more organizations optimize their customer-facing experiences to mobile websites and apps, DCS will become even more essential to create the optimal customer experience. Mobile devices do offer some interesting advantages over desktop DCS interactions. For instance, FaceID, thumbprints, and other biometrics can now be used to speed up the authentication process.

HOW DOES DCS COMPARE TO CCaaS?

Contact Center as a Service (CCaaS) is the term used to describe cloud-based software that powers contact center operations. It is traditionally a "phone-first" approach and offers *some* digital capabilities (typified by the "Digital-Also" approach described in Chapter 4).

DCS is effectively *digital-first CCaaS* since it powers the entirety of the contact center (including agents who are taking off-screen phone calls) by introducing OnScreen Enhancements to every interaction. At first, DCS will integrate with CCaaS, but eventually – as organizations strive to digitally transform customer service – DCS will likely replace the CCaaS system.

HOW DOES DCS COMPARE TO AN "OMNI-CHANNEL" CONTACT CENTER?

An *omni-channel* contact center would be defined as one that offers a variety of options beyond telephony-based contact (chat, email, social, for instance). As such, the contact center is practicing "digital customer service" but it may or may not be achieving true DCS. Vendors that provide omni-channel contact center solutions are mainly phone centric, and the challenge is that digital enhancements are offered in a "bolt-on" fashion. As such, the customer often has to disconnect from one interaction type (such as chat) to start another interaction type (such as voice or video).

DCS platforms are built from the ground up to support digital interaction types. In order for the predominant modality of contact to be considered DCS, OnScreen Enhancements must be available for every type of interaction and the contact center must be focused on "meeting customers where they are" in the midst of their already-digital interaction. Another important aspect of DCS is the ability to move between interaction modes seamlessly, which may not be possible in an omni-channel contact center.

HOW DOES WFM / WFO (WORKFORCE MANAGEMENT / OPTIMIZATION) FIT IN A DCS WORLD?

Most WFM solutions work well with DCS solutions via standard APIs. WFM solutions can get the scheduling data they need from the DCS system. Since DCS agents are generally deployed to handle all types of modalities (text, voice, video), scheduling the workforce is simplified compared to an omni-channel contact center.

WFO solutions can be modified to treat text, voice, and video part of interaction as one engagement. With this modification, analytics and QA processes can be handled as usual with text. Voice and video insights that include a combination of text, voice, and video interactions are available at the engagement level.

HOW WILL IVR TECHNOLOGY CHANGE WITH DCS?

The need for IVR will dissipate as interactions move to DCS. All of the routing, authentication and context formerly offered by those systems will become automated. There is no longer a need to ask a customer if they are looking for Sales or Service, or to enter their customer number, as all of that information can be gathered from their screen experience before the customer ever asks to speak to a representative. As more and more customers use DCS, fewer customers will begin an interaction through IVR.

HOW DOES DCS FIT IN WITH AN ON-PREMISES CALL CENTER?

DCS is not inherently a cloud-based offering (although the best solutions tend to be available as cloud deployments) and can co-exist with an on-prem call center. There are certainly "digital-also" options for DCS that can be utilized by on-prem contact centers and, if the organization is open to it, there are options to offer OnScreen Enhancements from the cloud in an on-prem environment as well.

WHAT ARE SECURITY, PRIVACY, AND COMPLIANCE CONSIDERATIONS FOR DCS?

In a DCS environment, the possibility of data theft is minimized to the lowest level of risk. For instance, an agent should never have to directly request a customer's personal data, because by the time an agent enters an interaction with a customer, that person has likely already been authenticated through the company's website or mobile app. In addition, any text a customer enters is displayed to the agent in real time, but sensitive personal information is automatically masked. Overall, higher levels of data security are achieved by enabling the customer to remain in the digital journey they have already initiated – instead of switching to another system.

HOW WILL AR/VR OR FUTURE TECHNOLOGY CHANGE DCS?

Because DCS is a system that supports customers on their screen instead of the phone, it is a future-proof framework. Newer technologies like AR/VR are simply another screen or entry point where organizations are able to meet the customer. By incorporating OnScreen Collaboration, Automation, and Communication from within AR/VR, it is possible to extend DCS to these experiences.

Notes

PREFACE: NOW IT'S OUR TURN

1. Craig Lee, "Screen Zombies: Average Person Will Spend 44 Hours Looking at Devices – and That's before Covid!" *Study Finds* (December 26, 2020), https://www.studyfinds.org/screen-zombies-average-person-spends-44-years-looking-at-devices/#:~:text=NEW%20YORK%20%E2%80%94%20As%20millions%20of,some%20kind%20of%20digital%20screen.

CHAPTER 2: THE PEAKS AND VALLEYS OF CUSTOMER SERVICE

1. *Customer baggage* – term coined by Lara Ponomareff, Corporate Executive Board.
2. John Goodman, *2020 National Customer Rage Study.* Customer Care Measurement & Consulting, 2020. https://www.customercaremc.com/insights/national-customer-rage-study/2020-national-customer-rage-study/
3. Anthony Dukes and Yi Zhu, "Why Is Customer Service So Bad? Because It's Profitable." *Harvard Business Review* (February 28, 2019), https://hbr.org/2019/02/why-is-customer-service-so-bad-because-its-profitable (accessed March 13, 2021).
4. "Why Call Centers Once are Coming Back to the US," Datamark Incorporated, https://insights.datamark.net/why-call-centers-once-outsourced-overseas-are-coming-back-to-the-u-s/(accessed March 3, 2021).

5. "Call Center Pricing," WorldWide Call Centers, Inc., https://www.worldwidecallcenter.com/call-center-pricing (accessed March 14, 2021).

6. "Who's Answering Your Customer Service Calls," Replicant (May 14, 2021), https://www.replicant.ai/whos-answering-your-customer-service-calls/ (accessed March 15, 2021).

CHAPTER 3: DIGITAL SELF-SERVICE CHANGED THINGS FOREVER

1. "A History of ATM Innovation," NCR (January 12, 2021), https://www.ncr.com/blogs/banking/history-atm-innovation (accessed February 21, 2021).

2. Anna Gedal, "How a Blizzard Changed Banking." New York Historical Society (March 21, 2016), https://behindthescenes.nyhistory.org/blizzard-changed-banking/ (accessed February 21, 2021).

3. Ibid.

4. "The Evolution of Customer Service Technology," WhosOn, https://www.whoson.com/customer-service/the-evolution-of-customer-service-technology/ (accessed February 21, 2021).

5. Shep Hyken, *The Convenience Revolution: How to Deliver a Customer Service Experience That Disrupts the Competition and Creates Fierce Loyalty* (Shippensburg, PA: Sound Wisdom Publishing, 2018).

6. Paul Napper and Anthony Rao, *The Power of Agency: The 7 Principles to Conquer Obstacles, Make Effective Decisions, and Create a Life on Your Own Terms* (New York: St. Martin's Press, 2019).

7. John Goodman, *2020 National Customer Rage Study*. Customer Care Measurement & Consulting, 2020. https://www.customercaremc.com/insights/national-customer-rage-study/2020-national-customer-rage-study/

8. Nicole Martin, "Why Millenials Have Higher Expectations for Customer Experience than Older Generations," Forbes (March 26, 2019), https://www.forbes.com/sites/nicolemartin1/2019/03/26/why-millennials-have-higher-expectations-for-customer-experience-than-older-generations (accessed February 12, 2021).

9. Jennifer Lund, "How Customer Experience Drives Digital Transformation," SuperOffice (May 4, 2021), https://www.superoffice.com/blog/digital-transformation/ (accessed March 25, 2021).

CHAPTER 5: THE PROCESS – A STEP-BY-STEP GUIDE

1. "Mobile Fact Sheet," Pew Research Center (April 7, 2021), https://www.pewresearch.org/internet/fact-sheet/mobile/; Pew Research Center Research and Technology Mobile Fact Sheet, June 12, 2019. Accessed March 15, 2021.

CHAPTER 7: THE POSITIONING – HOW DCS FUTURE-PROOFS YOUR COMPANY

1. Daniel C. Schlenoff, "The Motor Vehicle, 1917," *Scientific American* (January 1, 2017), https://www.scientificamerican.com/article/the-motor-vehicle-1917-slide-show/.
2. Aaron Smith, "Record Shares of Americans Now Own Smart Phones, Have Home Broadband," Pew Research Center (January 12, 2017), https://www.pewresearch.org/fact-tank/2017/01/12/evolution-of-technology/ (accessed March 29, 2021).
3. Matthew Dixon, Nick Toman, Rick Delisi, *The Effortless Experience: Conquering the New Battleground for Customer Loyalty* (New York: Penguin Group, 2013).

Index